Ninja Woodfire Outdoor Grill & Smoker Cookbook 2023

1600 Days of Simple and Scrumptious Ninja Woodfire Grill & Smoker Recipes for BBQs, Parties, Gatherings, Weeknight Dinners, Family Meals, and More

Joan D. Jones

CONTENTS

Meatless 68

Introduction

Hello, my name is Joan D. Jones, and I am a passionate food enthusiast and an avid grill and smoker. I have spent the past several years exploring different types of grilling and smoking techniques, experimenting with various ingredients, and perfecting my recipes. After numerous requests from family and friends to share my recipes, I decided to compile them into a cookbook.

The Ninja Woodfire Outdoor Grill & Smoker Cookbook 2023: 1600 Days of Simple and Scrumptious Ninja Woodfire Grill & Smoker Recipes for BBQs, Parties, Gatherings, Weeknight Dinners, Family Meals, and More is the result of my hard work and dedication. This cookbook features 1600 days worth of easy-to-follow recipes that are perfect for any occasion, from backyard barbecues to weeknight dinners and everything in between.

What sets this cookbook apart is that it focuses on using the Ninja Woodfire Grill & Smoker, which is a versatile and efficient cooking tool that can be used to grill, smoke, and roast a wide range of foods. The recipes in this cookbook are designed to showcase the unique capabilities of the Ninja Woodfire Grill & Smoker, while also providing delicious and satisfying meals for any occasion.

One of the key advantages of this coo

kbook is its simplicity. The recipes are easy to follow and require minimal preparation time, making them perfect for busy individuals and families. Additionally, the ingredients used in these recipes are readily available and affordable, so you don't have to break the bank to enjoy delicious meals.

Another advantage of this cookbook is its versatility. The recipes are suitable for all types of diets and preferences, including vegetarian, vegan, and gluten-free options. Whether you're looking for a quick and easy meal or a show-stopping dish for a special occasion, this cookbook has something for everyone.

Whether you're a seasoned grill master or a beginner, the Ninja Woodfire Outdoor Grill & Smoker Cookbook 2023 will help you take your grilling and smoking skills to the next level.

What is Ninja Woodfire Outdoor Grill & Smoker exactly?

Ninja Woodfire Outdoor Grill & Smoker is a type of outdoor cooking equipment that allows you to grill, smoke, and cook food using wood as a fuel source. It features a firebox where the wood is burned, and the smoke and heat are drawn into the cooking chamber, which is where the food is placed. The Ninja Woodfire Outdoor Grill & Smoker is designed to give food a smoky, wood-fired flavor that is similar to that of traditional barbecue. It is typically made of high-quality materials such as stainless steel, and it may come with additional features such as temperature control, ash removal systems, and built-in thermometers.

Are the Ninja Woodfire Outdoor Grill & Smoker recipes easy to follow?

Yes, the Ninja Woodfire Outdoor Grill & Smoker recipes are generally easy to follow, and there are several reasons why this is the case:

Step-by-step instructions: Most Ninja Woodfire Outdoor Grill & Smoker recipes come with clear and concise step-by-step instructions that are easy to follow. These instructions guide the cook through each stage of the cooking process and ensure that the dish turns out perfectly.

User-friendly design: The Ninja Woodfire Outdoor Grill & Smoker is designed to be user-friendly, with intuitive controls and easy-to-read displays. This makes it easy for even novice cooks to operate and control the cooking process.

Wide range of recipes: There is a wide range of Ninja Woodfire Outdoor Grill & Smoker recipes available, from simple grilled meats and vegetables to more complex dishes like smoked ribs and brisket. This means that there is something for every taste and skill level.

What types of food can be cooked using the Ninja Woodfire Outdoor Grill & Smoker?

The Ninja Woodfire Outdoor Grill & Smoker is a versatile outdoor cooking equipment that can be used to cook a wide variety of foods. Here are some of the most popular types of food that can be cooked using the Ninja Woodfire Outdoor Grill & Smoker:

- **Meat**

The Ninja Woodfire Outdoor Grill & Smoker is perfect for cooking all kinds of meats, including beef, pork, chicken, and fish. Whether you want to grill a steak, smoke a brisket, or roast a whole chicken, the Ninja Woodfire Outdoor Grill & Smoker can handle it all.

- **Vegetables**

Grilling vegetables on the Ninja Woodfire Outdoor Grill & Smoker is a great way to add a smoky, charred flavor to your favorite veggies. Popular vegetables to grill include corn on the cob, zucchini, mushrooms, onions, and peppers.

- **Pizza**

Believe it or not, you can cook pizza on the Ninja Woodfire Outdoor Grill & Smoker. Simply place the pizza directly on the grill grates or use a pizza stone, and you'll have a delicious wood-fired pizza in no time.

- **Baked Goods**

The Ninja Woodfire Outdoor Grill & Smoker can also be used to bake a variety of goods, including bread, cakes, and even cookies. Simply use a cast-iron skillet or Dutch oven to bake your favorite recipes.

- **Desserts**

The Ninja Woodfire Outdoor Grill & Smoker is also great for making desserts like fruit crisps, cobblers, and even s'mores.

In addition to these foods, the Ninja Woodfire Outdoor Grill & Smoker can be used to cook a variety of other dishes, including stews, chili, and even paella. With a little creativity, there's no limit to what you can cook using this versatile outdoor cooking equipment.

Is the Ninja Woodfire Outdoor Grill & Smoker easy to clean?

The Ninja Woodfire Outdoor Grill & Smoker is generally easy to clean, although the cleaning process may vary depending on the specific model and the type of food that was cooked. Here are some tips for cleaning the Ninja Woodfire Outdoor Grill & Smoker:

- **Clean the grates:** The grates are the most important part of the grill to clean, as they come into contact with the food. Use a grill brush or scraper to remove any food particles or debris from the grates. For tougher stains, you can soak the grates in a mixture of warm water and dish soap for a few minutes before scrubbing them clean.

- **Empty the ash pan:** The ash pan is located beneath the firebox and collects the ashes and debris from the burned wood. Once the grill has cooled down, remove the ash pan and empty the contents into a trash can. You can then wash the ash pan with warm water and soap, and then dry it before replacing it in the grill.

- **Wipe down the exterior:** Use a damp cloth or sponge to wipe down the exterior of the grill, including the lid and the body. You can use mild soap if necessary, but be sure to rinse the grill thoroughly afterwards.

- **Check the grease tray:** Some models of the Ninja Woodfire Outdoor Grill & Smoker come with a grease tray that collects the drippings from the food. Be sure to empty the grease tray regularly to prevent buildup and potential fire hazards.

- **Store the grill properly:** To keep the grill in good condition and prevent rust, be sure to store it in a dry place when not in use. Covering the grill with a weather-resistant cover can also help to protect it from the elements.

The Ninja Woodfire Outdoor Grill & Smoker is relatively easy to clean, and regular cleaning can help to extend the life of the grill and ensure that it continues to perform well over time.

Breakfastst

Fast Coffee Donuts

Servings: 6
Cooking Time: 6 Minutes
Ingredients:
- ¼ cup sugar
- ½ teaspoon salt
- 1 cup flour
- 1 teaspoon baking powder
- ¼ cup coffee
- 1 tablespoon aquafaba
- 1 tablespoon sunflower oil

Directions:
1. In a large bowl, combine the sugar, salt, flour, and baking powder.
2. Add the coffee, aquafaba, and sunflower oil and mix until a dough is formed. Leave the dough to rest in and the refrigerator.
3. Insert the Crisper Basket and close the hood. Select AIR CRISP, set the temperature to 400ºF, and set the time to 6 minutes. Select START/STOP to begin preheating.
4. Remove the dough from the fridge and divide up, kneading each section into a doughnut.
5. Put the doughnuts in the basket. Close the hood and AIR CRISP for 6 minutes.
6. Serve immediately.

Grit And Ham Fritters

Servings: 6 To 8
Cooking Time: 20 Minutes
Ingredients:
- 4 cups water
- 1 cup quick-cooking grits
- ¼ teaspoon salt
- 2 tablespoons butter
- 2 cups grated Cheddar cheese, divided
- 1 cup finely diced ham
- 1 tablespoon chopped chives
- Salt and freshly ground black pepper, to taste
- 1 egg, beaten
- 2 cups panko bread crumbs
- Cooking spray

Directions:
1. Bring the water to a boil in a saucepan. Whisk in the grits and ¼ teaspoon of salt, and cook for 7 minutes until the grits are soft. Remove the pan from the heat and stir in the butter and 1 cup of the grated Cheddar cheese. Transfer the grits to a bowl and let them cool for 10 to 15 minutes.
2. Stir the ham, chives and the rest of the cheese into the grits and season with salt and pepper to taste. Add the beaten egg and refrigerate the mixture for 30 minutes.
3. Put the panko bread crumbs in a shallow dish. Measure out ¼-cup portions of the grits mixture and shape them into patties. Coat all sides of the patties with the panko bread crumbs, patting them with the hands so the crumbs adhere to the patties. You should have about 16 patties. Spritz both sides of the patties with cooking spray.
4. Insert the Crisper Basket and close the hood. Select AIR CRISP, set the temperature to 400ºF, and set the time to 12 minutes. Select START/STOP to begin preheating.
5. Place the fritters in the basket. Close the hood and AIR CRISP for 8 minutes. Using a flat spatula, flip the fritters over and AIR CRISP for another 4 minutes.
6. Serve hot.

Bacon And Broccoli Bread Pudding

Servings: 2 To 4
Cooking Time: 48 Minutes
Ingredients:

- ½ pound thick cut bacon, cut into ¼-inch pieces
- 3 cups brioche bread, cut into ½-inch cubes
- 2 tablespoons butter, melted
- 3 eggs
- 1 cup milk
- ½ teaspoon salt
- Freshly ground black pepper, to taste
- 1 cup frozen broccoli florets, thawed and chopped
- 1½ cups grated Swiss cheese

Directions:

1. Insert the Crisper Basket and close the hood. Select AIR CRISP, set the temperature to 400ºF, and set the time to 10 minutes. Select START/STOP to begin preheating.
2. Put the bacon in the basket. Close the hood and AIR CRISP for 8 minutes until crispy, shaking the basket a few times to help it cook evenly. Remove the bacon and set it aside on a paper towel.
3. AIR CRISP the brioche bread cubes for 2 minutes to dry and toast lightly.
4. Butter a cake pan. Combine all the remaining ingredients in a large bowl and toss well. Transfer the mixture to the buttered cake pan, cover with aluminum foil and refrigerate the bread pudding overnight, or for at least 8 hours.
5. Remove the cake pan from the refrigerator an hour before you plan to bake and let it sit on the countertop to come to room temperature.
6. Select BAKE, set the temperature to 330ºF, and set the time to 40 minutes. Select START/STOP to begin preheating.
7. Place the covered cake pan directly in the pot. Fold the ends of the aluminum foil over the top of the pan. Close the hood and BAKE for 20 minutes. Remove the foil and bake for an additional 20 minutes. If the top browns a little too much before the custard has set, simply return the foil to the pan. The bread pudding has cooked through when a skewer inserted into the center comes out clean.
8. Serve warm.

Spinach, Leek And Cheese Frittata

Servings: 2
Cooking Time: 20 To 23 Minutes
Ingredients:

- 4 large eggs
- 4 ounces baby bella mushrooms, chopped
- 1 cup baby spinach, chopped
- ½ cup shredded Cheddar cheese
- ⅓ cup chopped leek, white part only
- ¼ cup halved grape tomatoes
- 1 tablespoon 2% milk
- ¼ teaspoon dried oregano
- ¼ teaspoon garlic powder
- ½ teaspoon kosher salt
- Freshly ground black pepper, to taste
- Cooking spray

Directions:

1. Select BAKE, set the temperature to 300ºF, and set the time to 23 minutes. Select START/STOP to begin preheating.
2. Lightly spritz a baking pan with cooking spray.
3. Whisk the eggs in a large bowl until frothy. Add the mushrooms, baby spinach, cheese, leek, tomatoes, milk, oregano, garlic powder, salt, and pepper and stir until well blended. Pour the mixture into the prepared baking pan.
4. Place the pan directly in the pot. Close the hood and BAKE for 20 to 23 minutes, or until the center is puffed up and the top is golden brown.
5. Let the frittata cool for 5 minutes before slicing to serve.

Coconut Brown Rice Porridge With Dates

Servings: 1 Or 2
Cooking Time: 23 Minutes
Ingredients:
- ½ cup cooked brown rice
- 1 cup canned coconut milk
- ¼ cup unsweetened shredded coconut
- ¼ cup packed dark brown sugar
- 4 large Medjool dates, pitted and roughly chopped
- ½ teaspoon kosher salt
- ¼ teaspoon ground cardamom
- Heavy cream, for serving (optional)

Directions:
1. Select BAKE, set the temperature to 375°F, and set the time to 23 minutes. Select START/STOP to begin preheating.
2. Place all the ingredients except the heavy cream in a baking pan and stir until blended.
3. Place the pan directly in the pot. Close the hood and BAKE for 23 minutes until the porridge is thick and creamy. Stir the porridge halfway through the cooking time.
4. Remove from the grill and ladle the porridge into bowls.
5. Serve hot with a drizzle of the cream, if desired.

Ham And Cheese Cups

Servings:12
Cooking Time: 20 Minutes
Ingredients:
- 12 large eggs
- 3 tablespoons avocado oil
- 12 slices deli ham
- 1 cup shredded cheese of choice
- Salt
- Freshly ground black pepper

Directions:
1. Insert the Grill Grate and close the hood. Select GRILL, set the temperature to HI, and set the time to 20 minutes. Select START/STOP to begin preheating.
2. While the unit is preheating, in a large bowl, beat the eggs. Brush the avocado oil in the bottom and on the sides of two 6-cup muffin tins. Line each muffin cup with a slice of ham. Spoon the eggs evenly into each cup. Top with the shredded cheese and season with salt and pepper.
3. When the unit beeps to signify it has preheated, place one muffin tin on the Grill Grate. Close the hood and grill for 10 minutes.
4. After 10 minutes, open the hood and remove the muffin tin. Place the second muffin tin on the Grill Grate, close the hood, and cook for 10 minutes.
5. When cooking is complete, remove the cups from the tins and serve.

Banana Bread

Servings:3
Cooking Time: 22 Minutes
Ingredients:
- 3 ripe bananas, mashed
- 1 cup sugar
- 1 large egg
- 4 tablespoons (½ stick) unsalted butter, melted
- 1½ cups all-purpose flour
- 1 teaspoon baking soda
- 1 teaspoon salt

Directions:
1. Coat the insides of 3 mini loaf pans with cooking spray.
2. In a large mixing bowl, mix the bananas and sugar.
3. In a separate large mixing bowl, combine the egg, butter, flour, baking soda, and salt and mix well.
4. Add the banana mixture to the egg and flour mixture. Mix well.
5. Divide the batter evenly among the prepared pans.
6. Select BAKE, set the temperature to 310ºF, and set the time to 22 minutes. Select START/STOP to begin preheating.
7. Set the mini loaf pans into the pot.
8. Close the hood and BAKE for 22 minutes. Insert a toothpick into the center of each loaf; if it comes out clean, they are done.
9. When the loaves are cooked through, remove the pans from the Crisper Basket. Turn out the loaves onto a wire rack to cool.
10. Serve warm.

Brie And Apple Tart

Servings: 4
Cooking Time: 10 Minutes
Ingredients:
- 1 sheet ready-to-bake puff pastry (thawed, if frozen)
- 1 small apple, cored and thinly sliced
- 3 tablespoons honey
- 1 teaspoon light brown sugar, packed
- 1 (8-ounce) round Brie cheese
- 2 tablespoons unsalted butter, melted

Directions:
1. Insert the Grill Grate and close the hood. Select GRILL, set the temperature to LO, and set the time to 10 minutes. Select START/STOP to begin preheating.
2. While the unit is preheating, unroll the pastry dough on a flat surface. Place the apple slices in the center of the dough. Drizzle the honey over the apples and sprinkle the brown sugar on top. Unwrap the Brie and place it on top of the apple slices. Fold the ends of the pastry around the Brie, similar to wrapping up a package, making sure to fully enclose the Brie and apples. Using a basting brush, brush the pastry all over with the melted butter.
3. When the unit beeps to signify it has preheated, place the pastry on the grill. Close the hood and grill for 10 minutes.
4. When cooking is complete, the pastry will be a nice golden brown. The Brie may leak out while cooking, and this is okay. The filling will be hot, so be sure to let it cool for a few minutes before serving.

Veggie Frittata

Servings: 4
Cooking Time: 8 To 12 Minutes
Ingredients:

- ½ cup chopped red bell pepper
- ⅓ cup grated carrot
- ⅓ cup minced onion
- 1 teaspoon olive oil
- 1 egg
- 6 egg whites
- ⅓ cup 2% milk
- 1 tablespoon shredded Parmesan cheese

Directions:
1. Select BAKE, set the temperature to 350ºF, and set the time to 12 minutes. Select START/STOP to begin preheating.
2. Mix together the red bell pepper, carrot, onion, and olive oil in a baking pan and stir to combine.
3. Place the pan directly in the pot. Close the hood and BAKE for 4 to 6 minutes, or until the veggies are soft. Stir once during cooking.
4. Meantime, whisk together the egg, egg whites, and milk in a medium bowl until creamy.
5. When the veggies are done, pour the egg mixture over the top. Scatter with the Parmesan cheese.
6. Bake for an additional 4 to 6 minutes, or until the eggs are set and the top is golden around the edges.
7. Allow the frittata to cool for 5 minutes before slicing and serving.

Country-fried Steak And Eggs

Servings: 4
Cooking Time: 16 Minutes
Ingredients:

- For the country-fried steak
- 1 cup milk
- 2 large eggs
- 2 cups all-purpose flour
- 2 teaspoons salt
- 1 teaspoon freshly ground black pepper
- 1 teaspoon garlic powder
- 1 teaspoon onion powder
- ¼ teaspoon cayenne pepper
- ¾ teaspoon paprika
- 4 (8-ounce) cube or round steaks
- For the eggs and gravy
- 4 to 8 large eggs
- 4 tablespoons (½ stick) unsalted butter
- 4 tablespoons all-purpose flour
- ½ cup heavy (whipping) cream
- ¼ teaspoon salt
- ¼ teaspoon freshly ground black pepper

Directions:
1. Create an assembly line with 3 shallow dishes. In the first dish, whisk together the milk and eggs. In the second dish, combine the flour, salt, black pepper, garlic powder, onion powder, cayenne pepper, and paprika. Place a steak in the flour mixture to coat both sides, then dip it into the egg mixture to coat both sides. Dip the steak back in the flour mixture, coating both sides. Place the coated steaks in the third shallow dish.
2. Insert the Grill Grate and close the hood. Select GRILL, set the temperature to HI, and set the time to 6 minutes. Select START/STOP to begin preheating.
3. When the unit beeps to signify it has preheated, place all 4 steaks on the Grill Grate. Close the hood and cook for 3 minutes.
4. After 3 minutes, open the hood and flip the steaks. Close the hood and cook for 3 minutes more.
5. When grilling is complete, transfer the steaks to a plate. Using grill mitts, remove the Grill Grate from the unit, leaving any excess fat drippings from the Grill Grate in the Cooking Pot.
6. Select AIR CRISP, set the temperature to 400°F, and set the time to 10 minutes. Select START/STOP and then press the PREHEAT button to skip preheating. Crack the eggs in the Cooking Pot. Close the hood and cook for 5 minutes, until the egg whites are opaque and firm. Remove the eggs from the pot.
7. Place the butter and flour in the Cooking Pot with the remaining fat drippings. Stir with a wooden spoon or silicone whisk until the butter has melted. Pour in the heavy cream and add the salt and pepper. Stir until completely mixed.
8. Close the hood and cook for 3 minutes. After 3 minutes, open the hood, stir the gravy, then close the hood to cook for 2 minutes more.
9. When cooking is complete, stir the gravy again and let it sit until you're ready to serve. To serve, pour the gravy over the country-fried steaks next to the eggs.

Egg And Avocado Burrito

Servings: 4
Cooking Time: 3 To 5 Minutes
Ingredients:

- 4 low-sodium whole-wheat flour tortillas
- Filling:
- 1 hard-boiled egg, chopped
- 2 hard-boiled egg whites, chopped
- 1 ripe avocado, peeled, pitted, and chopped
- 1 red bell pepper, chopped
- 1 slice low-sodium, low-fat American cheese, torn into pieces
- 3 tablespoons low-sodium salsa, plus additional for serving (optional)

Directions:

1. Insert the Crisper Basket and close the hood. Select AIR CRISP, set the temperature to 390ºF, and set the time to 5 minutes. Select START/STOP to begin preheating.
2. Make the filling: Combine the egg, egg whites, avocado, red bell pepper, cheese, and salsa in a medium bowl and stir until blended.
3. Assemble the burritos: Arrange the tortillas on a clean work surface and place ¼ of the prepared filling in the middle of each tortilla, leaving about 1½-inch on each end unfilled. Fold in the opposite sides of each tortilla and roll up. Secure with toothpicks through the center, if needed.
4. Transfer the burritos to the Crisper Basket. Close the hood and AIR CRISP for 3 to 5 minutes, or until the burritos are crisp and golden brown.
5. Allow to cool for 5 minutes and serve with salsa, if desired.

Grilled Sausage Mix

Servings: 4
Cooking Time: 22 Minutes
Ingredients:

- 8 mini bell peppers
- 2 heads radicchio, each cut into 6 wedges
- Canola oil, for brushing
- Sea salt, to taste
- Freshly ground black pepper, to taste
- 6 breakfast sausage links
- 6 hot or sweet Italian sausage links

Directions:

1. Insert the Grill Grate and close the hood. Select GRILL, set the temperature to MAX, and set the time to 22 minutes. Select START/STOP to begin preheating.
2. While the unit is preheating, brush the bell peppers and radicchio with the oil. Season with salt and black pepper.
3. When the unit beeps to signify it has preheated, place the bell peppers and radicchio on the Grill Grate; close the hood and GRILL for 10 minutes, without flipping.
4. Meanwhile, poke the sausages with a fork or knife and brush them with some of the oil.
5. After 10 minutes, remove the vegetables and set aside. Decrease the temperature to LOW. Place the sausages on the Grill Grate; close the hood and GRILL for 6 minutes.
6. Flip the sausages. Close the hood and GRILL for 6 minutes more. Remove the sausages from the Grill Grate.
7. Serve the sausages and vegetables on a large cutting board or serving tray.

Banana Churros With Oatmeal

Servings: 2
Cooking Time: 15 Minutes
Ingredients:

- For the Churros:
- 1 large yellow banana, peeled, cut in half lengthwise, then cut in half widthwise
- 2 tablespoons whole-wheat pastry flour
- ⅛ teaspoon sea salt
- 2 teaspoons oil (sunflower or melted coconut)
- 1 teaspoon water
- Cooking spray
- 1 tablespoon coconut sugar
- ½ teaspoon cinnamon
- For the Oatmeal:
- ¾ cup rolled oats
- 1½ cups water

Directions:

1. To make the churros
2. Put the 4 banana pieces in a medium-size bowl and add the flour and salt. Stir gently. Add the oil and water. Stir gently until evenly mixed. You may need to press some coating onto the banana pieces.
3. Spray the Crisper Basket with the oil spray. Put the banana pieces in the Crisper Basket and AIR CRISP for 5 minutes. Remove, gently turn over, and AIR CRISP for another 5 minutes or until browned.
4. In a medium bowl, add the coconut sugar and cinnamon and stir to combine. When the banana pieces are nicely browned, spray with the oil and place in the cinnamon-sugar bowl. Toss gently with a spatula to coat the banana pieces with the mixture.
5. To make the oatmeal
6. While the bananas are cooking, make the oatmeal. In a medium pot, bring the oats and water to a boil, then reduce to low heat. Simmer, stirring often, until all the water is absorbed, about 5 minutes. Put the oatmeal into two bowls.
7. Top the oatmeal with the coated banana pieces and serve immediately.

Ham And Corn Muffins

Servings:8
Cooking Time: 6 Minutes
Ingredients:

- ¾ cup yellow cornmeal
- ¼ cup flour
- 1½ teaspoons baking powder
- ¼ teaspoon salt
- 1 egg, beaten
- 2 tablespoons canola oil
- ½ cup milk
- ½ cup shredded sharp Cheddar cheese
- ½ cup diced ham

Directions:

1. Select BAKE, set the temperature to 390ºF, and set the time to 6 minutes. Select START/STOP to begin preheating.
2. In a medium bowl, stir together the cornmeal, flour, baking powder, and salt.
3. Add the egg, oil, and milk to dry ingredients and mix well.
4. Stir in shredded cheese and diced ham.
5. Divide batter among 8 parchment paper-lined muffin cups.
6. Put 4 filled muffin cups in the pot. Close the hood and BAKE for 5 minutes.
7. Reduce temperature to 330ºF and bake for 1 minute or until a toothpick inserted in center of the muffin comes out clean.
8. Repeat steps 6 and 7 to bake remaining muffins.
9. Serve warm.

Honey-lime Glazed Grilled Fruit Salad

Servings: 4
Cooking Time: 4 Minutes
Ingredients:

- ½ pound strawberries, washed, hulled and halved
- 1 can pineapple chunks, drained, juice reserved
- 2 peaches, pitted and sliced
- 6 tablespoons honey, divided
- 1 tablespoon freshly squeezed lime juice

Directions:

1. Insert the Grill Grate and close the hood. Select GRILL, set the temperature to MAX, and set the time to 4 minutes. Select START/STOP to begin preheating.
2. While the unit is preheating, combine the strawberries, pineapple, and peaches in a large bowl with 3 tablespoons of honey. Toss to coat evenly.
3. When the unit beeps to signify it has preheated, place the fruit on the Grill Grate. Gently press the fruit down to maximize grill marks. Close the hood and GRILL for 4 minutes without flipping.
4. Meanwhile, in a small bowl, combine the remaining 3 tablespoons of honey, lime juice, and 1 tablespoon of reserved pineapple juice.
5. When cooking is complete, place the fruit in a large bowl and toss with the honey mixture. Serve immediately.

Chicken Breakfast Sausages

Servings: 8
Cooking Time: 8 To 12 Minutes
Ingredients:

- 1 Granny Smith apple, peeled and finely chopped
- 2 tablespoons apple juice
- 2 garlic cloves, minced
- 1 egg white
- ⅓ cup minced onion
- 3 tablespoons ground almonds
- ⅛ teaspoon freshly ground black pepper
- 1 pound ground chicken breast

Directions:

1. Insert the Crisper Basket and close the hood. Select AIR CRISP, set the temperature to 330ºF, and set the time to 12 minutes. Select START/STOP to begin preheating.
2. Combine all the ingredients except the chicken in a medium mixing bowl and stir well.
3. Add the chicken breast to the apple mixture and mix with your hands until well incorporated.
4. Divide the mixture into 8 equal portions and shape into patties. Arrange the patties in the Crisper Basket. You may need to work in batches depending on the size of your Crisper Basket.
5. Close the hood and AIR CRISP for 8 to 12 minutes, or until a meat thermometer inserted in the center of the chicken reaches at least 165ºF.
6. Remove from the grill to a plate and repeat with the remaining patties.
7. Let the chicken cool for 5 minutes and serve warm.

Pesto Egg Croissantwiches

Servings: 4
Cooking Time: 8 Minutes
Ingredients:

- 4 large eggs
- 4 croissants
- 8 tablespoons pesto

Directions:

1. Insert the Cooking Pot and close the hood. Select GRILL, set the temperature to HI, and set the time to 8 minutes. Select START/STOP to begin preheating.
2. While the unit is preheating, in a small bowl, whisk together the eggs.
3. When the unit beeps to signify it has preheated, pour the beaten eggs into the Cooking Pot. Close the hood and cook for 4 minutes.
4. While the eggs are cooking, split the croissants. Place the croissant halves on top of the Grill Grate.
5. After 4 minutes, open the hood and scramble the eggs with a spatula. Spoon the scrambled eggs onto the bottom halves of the croissants. Remove the Cooking Pot from the unit.
6. Insert the Grill Grate into the unit. Spoon 2 tablespoons of pesto on top of each egg-topped croissant, then top each sandwich with the croissant top. Close the hood and cook for 4 minutes.
7. When cooking is complete, the croissant crust should be toasted. Serve.

Maple Walnut Pancake

Servings: 4
Cooking Time: 20 Minutes
Ingredients:

- 3 tablespoons melted butter, divided
- 1 cup flour
- 2 tablespoons sugar
- 1½ teaspoons baking powder
- ¼ teaspoon salt
- 1 egg, beaten
- ¾ cup milk
- 1 teaspoon pure vanilla extract
- ½ cup roughly chopped walnuts
- Maple syrup or fresh sliced fruit, for serving

Directions:

1. Select BAKE, set the temperature to 330ºF, and set the time to 20 minutes. Select START/STOP to begin preheating.
2. Grease a baking pan with 1 tablespoon of melted butter.
3. Mix together the flour, sugar, baking powder, and salt in a medium bowl. Add the beaten egg, milk, the remaining 2 tablespoons of melted butter, and vanilla and stir until the batter is sticky but slightly lumpy.
4. Slowly pour the batter into the greased baking pan and scatter with the walnuts.
5. Place the pan directly in the pot. Close the hood and BAKE for 20 minutes until golden brown and cooked through.
6. Let the pancake rest for 5 minutes and serve topped with the maple syrup or fresh fruit, if desired.

Western Omelet

Servings: 2
Cooking Time: 18 To 21 Minutes
Ingredients:

- ¼ cup chopped bell pepper, green or red
- ¼ cup chopped onion
- ¼ cup diced ham
- 1 teaspoon butter
- 4 large eggs
- 2 tablespoons milk
- ⅛ teaspoon salt
- ¾ cup shredded sharp Cheddar cheese

Directions:

1. Select AIR CRISP, set the temperature to 390ºF, and set the time to 6 minutes. Select START/STOP to begin preheating.
2. Put the bell pepper, onion, ham, and butter in a baking pan and mix well. Place the pan directly in the pot.
3. Close the hood and AIR CRISP for 1 minute. Stir and continue to cook for an additional 4 to 5 minutes until the veggies are softened.
4. Meanwhile, whisk together the eggs, milk, and salt in a bowl.
5. Pour the egg mixture over the veggie mixture.
6. Reduce the grill temperature to 360ºF and BAKE for 13 to 15 minutes more, or until the top is lightly golden browned and the eggs are set.
7. Scatter the omelet with the shredded cheese. Bake for another 1 minute until the cheese has melted.
8. Let the omelet cool for 5 minutes before serving.

Asparagus And Cheese Strata

Servings: 4
Cooking Time: 14 To 19 Minutes
Ingredients:

- 6 asparagus spears, cut into 2-inch pieces
- 1 tablespoon water
- 2 slices whole-wheat bread, cut into ½-inch cubes
- 4 eggs
- 3 tablespoons whole milk
- 2 tablespoons chopped flat-leaf parsley
- ½ cup grated Havarti or Swiss cheese
- Pinch salt
- Freshly ground black pepper, to taste
- Cooking spray

Directions:

1. Select BAKE, set the temperature to 330ºF, and set the time to 19 minutes. Select START/STOP to begin preheating.
2. Add the asparagus spears and 1 tablespoon of water in a baking pan. Place the pan directly in the pot. Close the hood and BAKE for 3 to 5 minutes until crisp-tender. Remove the asparagus from the pan and drain on paper towels. Spritz the pan with cooking spray.
3. Place the bread and asparagus in the pan.
4. Whisk together the eggs and milk in a medium mixing bowl until creamy. Fold in the parsley, cheese, salt, and pepper and stir to combine. Pour this mixture into the baking pan.
5. Place the pan directly in the pot. Close the hood and BAKE for 11 to 14 minutes, or until the eggs are set and the top is lightly browned.
6. Let cool for 5 minutes before slicing and serving.

Mini Caprese Pizzas

Servings: 4
Cooking Time: 10 Minutes
Ingredients:

- 1 (14-ounce) package refrigerated pizza dough
- 2 tablespoons extra-virgin olive oil
- 2 large tomatoes, thinly sliced
- 8 ounces fresh mozzarella cheese, cut into thin discs
- 12 fresh basil leaves
- Balsamic vinegar, for drizzling or dipping

Directions:

1. Insert the Grill Grate and close the hood. Select GRILL, set the temperature to MED, and set the time to 10 minutes. Select START/STOP to begin preheating.
2. While the unit is preheating, lay the pizza dough on a flat surface. Cut out 12 small round pizzas 1½ to 2 inches diameter each. Brush both sides of each dough round with the olive oil.
3. When the unit beeps to signify it has preheated, place the dough rounds on the Grill Grate, 4 across, in 3 rows. Close the hood and grill for 5 minutes.
4. After 5 minutes, open the hood and flip the rounds. Top each round with the tomato and cheese slices. Close the hood and cook for 5 minutes more.
5. When cooking is complete, remove the pizzas from the Grill Grate. Top each with the basil. When ready to serve, drizzle each pizza with the balsamic vinegar, or keep the vinegar on the side in a small bowl for dipping.

Grilled Egg And Arugula Pizza

Servings: 2
Cooking Time: 8 Minutes
Ingredients:
- 2 tablespoons all-purpose flour, plus more as needed
- ½ store-bought pizza dough
- 1 tablespoon canola oil, divided
- 1 cup fresh ricotta cheese
- 4 large eggs
- Sea salt, to taste
- Freshly ground black pepper, to taste
- 4 cups arugula, torn
- 1 tablespoon extra-virgin olive oil
- 1 teaspoon freshly squeezed lemon juice
- 2 tablespoons grated Parmesan cheese

Directions:
1. Insert the Grill Grate and close the hood. Select GRILL, set the temperature to MAX, and set the time to 7 minutes. Select START/STOP to begin preheating.
2. While the unit is preheating, dust a clean work surface with flour. Place the dough on the floured surface and roll it into a 9-inch round of even thickness. Dust your rolling pin and work surface with additional flour, as needed, to ensure the dough does not stick.
3. Brush the surface of the rolled-out dough evenly with ½ tablespoon of canola oil. Flip the dough over and brush with the remaining ½ tablespoon oil. Poke the dough with a fork 5 or 6 times across its surface to prevent air pockets from forming during cooking.
4. When the unit beeps to signify it has preheated, place the dough on the Grill Grate. Close the hood and GRILL for 4 minutes.
5. After 4 minutes, flip the dough, then spoon teaspoons of ricotta cheese across the surface of the dough, leaving a 1-inch border around the edges.
6. Crack one egg into a ramekin or small bowl. This way you can easily remove any shell that may break into the egg and keep the yolk intact. Imagine the dough is split into four quadrants. Pour one egg into each. Repeat with the remaining 3 eggs. Season the pizza with salt and pepper.
7. Close the hood and continue cooking for the remaining 3 to 4 minutes until the egg whites are firm.
8. Meanwhile, in a medium bowl, toss together the arugula, oil, and lemon juice, and season with salt and pepper.
9. Transfer the pizza to a cutting board and let it cool. Top it with the arugula mixture, drizzle with olive oil, if desired, and sprinkle with Parmesan cheese. Cut into pieces and serve.

Spinach With Scrambled Eggs

Servings: 2
Cooking Time: 10 Minutes
Ingredients:
- 2 tablespoons olive oil
- 4 eggs, whisked
- 5 ounces fresh spinach, chopped
- 1 medium tomato, chopped
- 1 teaspoon fresh lemon juice
- ½ teaspoon coarse salt
- ½ teaspoon ground black pepper
- ½ cup of fresh basil, roughly chopped

Directions:
1. Grease a baking pan with the oil, tilting it to spread the oil around.
2. Select BAKE, set the temperature to 280°F, and set the time to 10 minutes. Select START/STOP to begin preheating.
3. In the pan, mix the remaining ingredients, apart from the basil leaves, whisking well until everything is completely combined.
4. Place the pan directly in the pot. Close the hood and BAKE for 10 minutes.
5. Top with fresh basil leaves before serving.

Grilled Kielbasa And Pineapple Kebabs

Servings: 4
Cooking Time: 12 Minutes
Ingredients:

- ½ cup soy sauce
- ¼ cup light brown sugar, packed
- 2 (8-ounce) cans pineapple chunks, drained
- 2 (12-ounce) packages kielbasa sausages, cut into ½-inch slices

Directions:

1. In a large bowl, mix together the soy sauce, brown sugar, and pineapple chunks until the sugar is dissolved. Add the sausage slices and set aside for 10 minutes.
2. Thread the kielbasa and pineapple onto 10 to 12 skewers, alternating meat and fruit. Set aside any glaze that remains in the bowl.
3. Insert the Grill Grate and close the hood. Select GRILL, set the temperature to HI, and set the time to 12 minutes. Select START/STOP to begin preheating.
4. When the unit beeps to signify it has preheated, place half of the skewers on the Grill Grate. Brush them with extra glaze. Close the hood and grill for 3 minutes.
5. After 3 minutes, open the hood and flip the skewers. Close the hood and cook for 3 minutes more. After a total of 6 minutes, remove the skewers. Repeat with the remaining skewers.
6. When cooking is complete, remove the skewers from the grill and serve.

Mushroom And Onion Frittata

Servings: 4
Cooking Time: 10 Minutes
Ingredients:

- 4 large eggs
- ¼ cup whole milk
- Sea salt, to taste
- Freshly ground black pepper, to taste
- ½ bell pepper, seeded and diced
- ½ onion, chopped
- 4 cremini mushrooms, sliced
- ½ cup shredded Cheddar cheese

Directions:

1. In a medium bowl, whisk together the eggs and milk. Season with the salt and pepper. Add the bell pepper, onion, mushrooms, and cheese. Mix until well combined.
2. Select BAKE, set the temperature to 400ºF, and set the time to 10 minutes. Select START/STOP to begin preheating.
3. Meanwhile, pour the egg mixture into the baking pan, spreading evenly.
4. When the unit beeps to signify it has preheated, place the pan directly in the pot. Close the hood and BAKE for 10 minutes, or until lightly golden.

English Pumpkin Egg Bake

Servings: 2
Cooking Time: 10 Minutes
Ingredients:

- 2 eggs
- ½ cup milk
- 2 cups flour
- 2 tablespoons cider vinegar
- 2 teaspoons baking powder
- 1 tablespoon sugar
- 1 cup pumpkin purée
- 1 teaspoon cinnamon powder
- 1 teaspoon baking soda
- 1 tablespoon olive oil

Directions:

1. Select BAKE, set the temperature to 300ºF, and set the time to 10 minutes. Select START/STOP to begin preheating.
2. Crack the eggs into a bowl and beat with a whisk. Combine with the milk, flour, cider vinegar, baking powder, sugar, pumpkin purée, cinnamon powder, and baking soda, mixing well.
3. Grease a baking pan with oil. Add the mixture to the pan. Place the pan directly in the pot. Close the hood and BAKE for 10 minutes.
4. Serve warm.

Soufflé

Servings: 4
Cooking Time: 22 Minutes
Ingredients:

- ⅓ cup butter, melted
- ¼ cup flour
- 1 cup milk
- 1 ounce sugar
- 4 egg yolks
- 1 teaspoon vanilla extract
- 6 egg whites
- 1 teaspoon cream of tartar
- Cooking spray

Directions:

1. In a bowl, mix the butter and flour until a smooth consistency is achieved.
2. Pour the milk into a saucepan over medium-low heat. Add the sugar and allow to dissolve before raising the heat to boil the milk.
3. Pour in the flour and butter mixture and stir rigorously for 7 minutes to eliminate any lumps. Make sure the mixture thickens. Take off the heat and allow to cool for 15 minutes.
4. Select BAKE, set the temperature to 320ºF, and set the time to 15 minutes. Select START/STOP to begin preheating.
5. Spritz 6 soufflé dishes with cooking spray.
6. Put the egg yolks and vanilla extract in a separate bowl and beat them together with a fork. Pour in the milk and combine well to incorporate everything.
7. In a smaller bowl mix the egg whites and cream of tartar with a fork. Fold into the egg yolks-milk mixture before adding in the flour mixture. Transfer equal amounts to the 6 soufflé dishes.
8. Put the dishes in the grill. Close the hood and BAKE for 15 minutes.
9. Serve warm.

Pb&j

Servings: 4
Cooking Time: 6 Minutes
Ingredients:

- ½ cup cornflakes, crushed
- ¼ cup shredded coconut
- 8 slices oat nut bread or any whole-grain, oversize bread
- 6 tablespoons peanut butter
- 2 medium bananas, cut into ½-inch-thick slices
- 6 tablespoons pineapple preserves
- 1 egg, beaten
- Cooking spray

Directions:

1. Insert the Crisper Basket and close the hood. Select AIR CRISP, set the temperature to 360ºF, and set the time to 6 minutes. Select START/STOP to begin preheating.
2. In a shallow dish, mix the cornflake crumbs and coconut.
3. For each sandwich, spread one bread slice with 1½ tablespoons of peanut butter. Top with banana slices. Spread another bread slice with 1½ tablespoons of preserves. Combine to make a sandwich.
4. Using a pastry brush, brush top of sandwich lightly with beaten egg. Sprinkle with about 1½ tablespoons of crumb coating, pressing it in to make it stick. Spray with cooking spray.
5. Turn sandwich over and repeat to coat and spray the other side. Place the sandwiches in the Crisper Basket.
6. Close the hood and AIR CRISP for 6 minutes or until coating is golden brown and crispy.
7. Cut the cooked sandwiches in half and serve warm.

Apple And Walnut Muffins

Servings:8
Cooking Time: 10 Minutes
Ingredients:

- 1 cup flour
- ⅓ cup sugar
- 1 teaspoon baking powder
- ¼ teaspoon baking soda
- ¼ teaspoon salt
- 1 teaspoon cinnamon
- ¼ teaspoon ginger
- ¼ teaspoon nutmeg
- 1 egg
- 2 tablespoons pancake syrup, plus 2 teaspoons
- 2 tablespoons melted butter, plus 2 teaspoons
- ¾ cup unsweetened applesauce
- ½ teaspoon vanilla extract
- ¼ cup chopped walnuts
- ¼ cup diced apple

Directions:

1. Select BAKE, set the temperature to 330ºF, and set the time to 10 minutes. Select START/STOP to begin preheating.
2. In a large bowl, stir together the flour, sugar, baking powder, baking soda, salt, cinnamon, ginger, and nutmeg.
3. In a small bowl, beat egg until frothy. Add syrup, butter, applesauce, and vanilla and mix well.
4. Pour egg mixture into dry ingredients and stir just until moistened.
5. Gently stir in nuts and diced apple.
6. Divide batter among 8 parchment paper-lined muffin cups.
7. Put 4 muffin cups in the pot. Close the hood and BAKE for 10 minutes.
8. Repeat with remaining 4 muffins or until toothpick inserted in center comes out clean.
9. Serve warm.

Mixed Berry Dutch Baby Pancake

Servings: 4
Cooking Time: 12 To 16 Minutes
Ingredients:

- 1 tablespoon unsalted butter, at room temperature
- 1 egg
- 2 egg whites
- ½ cup 2% milk
- ½ cup whole-wheat pastry flour
- 1 teaspoon pure vanilla extract
- 1 cup sliced fresh strawberries
- ½ cup fresh raspberries
- ½ cup fresh blueberries

Directions:

1. Select BAKE, set the temperature to 330ºF, and set the time to 16 minutes. Select START/STOP to begin preheating.
2. Grease a baking pan with the butter.
3. Using a hand mixer, beat together the egg, egg whites, milk, pastry flour, and vanilla in a medium mixing bowl until well incorporated.
4. Pour the batter into the pan. Place the pan directly in the pot. Close the hood and BAKE for 12 to 16 minutes, or until the pancake puffs up in the center and the edges are golden brown.
5. Allow the pancake to cool for 5 minutes and serve topped with the berries.

Sides, Snacks & Appetizers

Cheesy Steak Fries

Servings: 5
Cooking Time: 20 Minutes
Ingredients:
- 1 bag frozen steak fries
- Cooking spray
- Salt and pepper, to taste
- ½ cup beef gravy
- 1 cup shredded Mozzarella cheese
- 2 scallions, green parts only, chopped

Directions:
1. Insert the Crisper Basket and close the hood. Select AIR CRISP, set the temperature to 400ºF, and set the time to 20 minutes. Select START/STOP to begin preheating.
2. Place the frozen steak fries in the basket. Close the hood and AIR CRISP for 10 minutes. Shake the basket and spritz the fries with cooking spray. Sprinkle with salt and pepper. AIR CRISP for an additional 8 minutes.
3. Pour the beef gravy into a medium, microwave-safe bowl. Microwave for 30 seconds, or until the gravy is warm.
4. Sprinkle the fries with the cheese. Close the hood and AIR CRISP for an additional 2 minutes, until the cheese is melted.
5. Transfer the fries to a serving dish. Drizzle the fries with gravy and sprinkle the scallions on top for a green garnish. Serve.

Creamy Artichoke Dip With Pita Chips

Servings: 4
Cooking Time: 15 Minutes
Ingredients:
- 8 ounces cream cheese, at room temperature
- 1 (13-ounce) can marinated artichoke quarters, drained and coarsely chopped
- ½ cup sour cream
- ½ cup grated Parmesan cheese
- ¼ teaspoon garlic powder
- 2 cups shredded mozzarella
- 1 (6-ounce) package mini pita bread rounds
- Extra-virgin olive oil
- Chopped fresh chives, for garnish

Directions:
1. Insert the Cooking Pot and close the hood. Select GRILL, set the temperature to MED, and set the time to 15 minutes. Select START/STOP to begin preheating.
2. While the unit is preheating, place the cream cheese, artichokes, sour cream, Parmesan cheese, garlic powder, and mozzarella cheese in a 9-by-5-inch loaf pan. Stir until well combined.
3. When the unit beeps to signify it has preheated, place the pan in the Cooking Pot. Close the hood and cook for 5 minutes.
4. After 5 minutes, open the hood and stir the dip with a wooden spoon, holding onto the loaf pan with grill mitts. Close the hood and cook for 7 minutes more.
5. Meanwhile, place the Grill Grate next to the Foodi™ Grill. Put the pita rounds in a large bowl and drizzle with the olive oil. Toss to coat. Place the pita rounds on the Grill Grate.
6. After 7 minutes, open the hood. Remove the pan of artichoke dip from the Cooking Pot. Place the Grill Grate into the unit. Close the hood and cook for the remaining 3 minutes.
7. Cooking is complete when the pita chips are warm and crispy. Garnish the dip with the fresh chives and serve.

Roasted Mixed Nuts

Servings: 6
Cooking Time: 20 Minutes
Ingredients:
- 2 cups mixed nuts (walnuts, pecans, and almonds)
- 2 tablespoons egg white
- 2 tablespoons sugar
- 1 teaspoon paprika
- 1 teaspoon ground cinnamon
- Cooking spray

Directions:
1. Spray the Crisper Basket with cooking spray.
2. Insert the Crisper Basket and close the hood. Select ROAST, set the temperature to 300ºF, and set the time to 20 minutes. Select START/STOP to begin preheating.
3. Stir together the mixed nuts, egg white, sugar, paprika, and cinnamon in a small bowl until the nuts are fully coated.
4. Put the nuts in the Crisper Basket. Close the hood and ROAST for 20 minutes. Shake the basket halfway through the cooking time for even cooking.
5. Transfer the nuts to a bowl and serve warm.

Cheese And Ham Stuffed Baby Bella

Servings: 8
Cooking Time: 12 Minutes
Ingredients:
- 4 ounces Mozzarella cheese, cut into pieces
- ½ cup diced ham
- 2 green onions, chopped
- 2 tablespoons bread crumbs
- ½ teaspoon garlic powder
- ¼ teaspoon ground oregano
- ¼ teaspoon ground black pepper
- 1 to 2 teaspoons olive oil
- 16 fresh Baby Bella mushrooms, stemmed removed

Directions:
1. Process the cheese, ham, green onions, bread crumbs, garlic powder, oregano, and pepper in a food processor until finely chopped.
2. With the food processor running, slowly drizzle in 1 to 2 teaspoons olive oil until a thick paste has formed. Transfer the mixture to a bowl.
3. Evenly divide the mixture into the mushroom caps and lightly press down the mixture.
4. Insert the Crisper Basket and close the hood. Select ROAST, set the temperature to 390ºF, and set the time to 12 minutes. Select START/STOP to begin preheating.
5. Lay the mushrooms in the Crisper Basket in a single layer. You'll need to work in batches to avoid overcrowding.
6. Close the hood and ROAST for 12 minutes until the mushrooms are lightly browned and tender.
7. Remove from the basket to a plate and repeat with the remaining mushrooms.
8. Let the mushrooms cool for 5 minutes and serve warm.

Goat Cheese Bruschetta With Tomatoes

Servings: 4
Cooking Time: 8 Minutes
Ingredients:

- 8 ounces cherry tomatoes (about 35)
- 8 fresh basil leaves
- 1 tablespoon balsamic vinegar
- 1 (8-ounce) baguette
- ½ cup extra-virgin olive oil
- 2 tablespoons garlic powder
- 8 ounces goat cheese (unflavored)

Directions:

1. Insert the Grill Grate and close the hood. Select GRILL, set the temperature to HI, and set the time to 8 minutes. Select START/STOP to begin preheating.
2. While the unit is preheating, quarter the cherry tomatoes. Slice the basil leaves into very thin ribbons. Place the tomatoes and basil in a medium bowl. Add the balsamic vinegar and toss to coat.
3. Slice the baguette into ½-inch slices. In a small bowl, whisk together the olive oil and garlic powder. Brush both sides of the baguette slices with the olive oil mixture.
4. When the unit beeps to signify it has preheated, place half the baguette slices on the Grill Grate in a single layer. Close the hood and cook for 4 minutes. After 4 minutes, remove the baguettes from the grill and set aside on a plate. Place the remaining slices on the Grill Grate. Close the hood and cook for 4 minutes.
5. When cooking is complete, spread a layer of goat cheese on the baguette slices. Top with the tomato-basil mixture and serve.

Avocado Egg Rolls

Servings: 4
Cooking Time: 10 Minutes
Ingredients:

- 4 avocados, pitted and diced
- ½ white onion, diced
- ⅓ cup sun-dried tomatoes, chopped
- 1 (16-ounce) package egg roll wrappers (about 20 wrappers)
- ¼ cup water, for sealing
- 4 tablespoons avocado oil

Directions:

1. Insert the Grill Grate and close the hood. Select GRILL, set the temperature to LO, and set the time to 10 minutes. Select START/STOP to begin preheating.
2. While the unit is preheating, place the diced avocado in a large bowl. Add the onion and sun-dried tomatoes and gently fold together, being careful to not mash the avocado.
3. Place an egg roll wrapper on a flat surface with a corner facing you (like a diamond). Add 2 to 3 tablespoons of the filling in the center of the wrapper. The amount should be about 2½ inches wide. Gently lift the bottom corner of the wrapper over the filling, fold in the sides, and roll away from you to close. Dip your finger into the water and run it over the top corner of the wrapper to seal it. Continue filling, folding, and sealing the rest of the egg rolls.
4. When the unit beeps to signify it has preheated, brush the avocado oil on all sides of the egg rolls. Place the egg rolls on the Grill Grate, seam-side down. Close the hood and grill for 5 minutes.
5. After 5 minutes, open the hood and flip the egg rolls. Give them another brush of avocado oil. Close the hood and cook for 5 minutes more.
6. When cooking is complete, the wrappers will be golden brown. Remove from the grill and serve.

Breaded Green Olives

Servings: 4
Cooking Time: 8 Minutes
Ingredients:

- 1 jar pitted green olives
- ½ cup all-purpose flour
- Salt and pepper, to taste
- ½ cup bread crumbs
- 1 egg
- Cooking spray

Directions:

1. Insert the Crisper Basket and close the hood. Select AIR CRISP, set the temperature to 400ºF, and set the time to 8 minutes. Select START/STOP to begin preheating.
2. Remove the olives from the jar and dry thoroughly with paper towels.
3. In a small bowl, combine the flour with salt and pepper to taste. Place the bread crumbs in another small bowl. In a third small bowl, beat the egg.
4. Spritz the Crisper Basket with cooking spray.
5. Dip the olives in the flour, then the egg, and then the bread crumbs.
6. Place the breaded olives in the basket. It is okay to stack them. Spray the olives with cooking spray. Close the hood and AIR CRISP for 6 minutes. Flip the olives and AIR CRISP for an additional 2 minutes, or until brown and crisp.
7. Cool before serving.

Bacon-wrapped Onion Rings And Spicy Aioli

Servings: 4
Cooking Time: 10 Minutes
Ingredients:

- For the onion rings
- 3 large white onions
- 2 (1-pound) packages thin-sliced bacon
- For the spicy garlic aioli sauce
- 1 cup mayonnaise
- ¼ teaspoon garlic powder
- 1 tablespoon sriracha
- 1 teaspoon freshly squeezed lemon juice

Directions:

1. Insert the Grill Grate and close the hood. Select GRILL, set the temperature to MED, and set the time to 10 minutes. Select START/STOP to begin preheating.
2. While the unit is preheating, cut both ends off the onions. Slice each onion crosswise into thirds and peel off the outer layer of onion skin. Separate the onion rings, keeping two onion layers together to have a stable and firm ring. Wrap each onion ring pair with a slice of bacon. The bacon should slightly overlap itself as you wrap it all the way around the onion ring. Larger rings may need 2 slices of bacon.
3. When the unit beeps to signify it has preheated, place the onion rings on the Grill Grate. Close the hood and grill for 10 minutes. Flipping is not necessary.
4. When cooking is complete, the bacon will be cooked through and starting to crisp. If you prefer the bacon crispier or even close to charred, continue cooking to your liking.
5. While the onion rings are cooking, in a small bowl, whisk together the mayonnaise, garlic powder, sriracha, and lemon juice. Use more or less sriracha depending on your preferred spice level. Serve with the bacon onion rings.

Cheesy Crab Toasts

Servings: 15
Cooking Time: 5 Minutes
Ingredients:

- 1 can flaked crab meat, well drained
- 3 tablespoons light mayonnaise
- ¼ cup shredded Parmesan cheese
- ¼ cup shredded Cheddar cheese
- 1 teaspoon Worcestershire sauce
- ½ teaspoon lemon juice
- 1 loaf artisan bread, French bread, or baguette, cut into ⅜-inch-thick slices

Directions:

1. Insert the Crisper Basket and close the hood. Select BAKE, set the temperature to 360°F, and set the time to 5 minutes. Select START/STOP to begin preheating.
2. In a large bowl, stir together all the ingredients except the bread slices.
3. On a clean work surface, lay the bread slices. Spread ½ tablespoon of crab mixture onto each slice of bread.
4. Arrange the bread slices in the Crisper Basket in a single layer. You'll need to work in batches to avoid overcrowding.
5. Close the hood and BAKE for 5 minutes until the tops are lightly browned.
6. Transfer to a plate and repeat with the remaining bread slices.
7. Serve warm.

Crispy Spiced Potatoes

Servings: 4
Cooking Time: 20 Minutes
Ingredients:

- 2 pounds baby red potatoes, quartered
- 2 tablespoons extra-virgin olive oil
- ¼ cup dried onion flakes
- 1 teaspoon dried rosemary
- ½ teaspoon onion powder
- ½ teaspoon garlic powder
- ¼ teaspoon celery powder
- ¼ teaspoon freshly ground black pepper
- ½ teaspoon dried parsley
- ½ teaspoon sea salt

Directions:

1. Insert the Crisper Basket and close the hood. Select AIR CRISP, set the temperature to 390°F, and set the time to 20 minutes. Select START/STOP to begin preheating.
2. Meanwhile, place all the ingredients in a large bowl and toss until evenly coated.
3. When the unit beeps to signify it has preheated, add the potatoes to the basket. Close the hood and AIR CRISP for 10 minutes.
4. After 10 minutes, shake the basket well. Place the basket back in the unit and close the hood to resume cooking.
5. After 10 minutes, check for desired crispness. Continue cooking up to 5 minutes more, if necessary.

Balsamic Broccoli

Servings: 4
Cooking Time: 10 Minutes
Ingredients:

- 4 tablespoons soy sauce
- 4 tablespoons balsamic vinegar
- 2 tablespoons canola oil
- 2 teaspoons maple syrup
- 2 heads broccoli, trimmed into florets
- Red pepper flakes, for garnish
- Sesame seeds, for garnish

Directions:

1. Insert the Grill Grate and close the hood. Select GRILL, set the temperature to MAX, and set the time to 10 minutes. Select START/STOP to begin preheating.
2. While the unit is preheating, in a large bowl, whisk together the soy sauce, balsamic vinegar, oil, and maple syrup. Add the broccoli and toss to coat evenly.
3. When the unit beeps to signify it has preheated, place the broccoli on the Grill Grate. Close the hood and GRILL for 8 to 10 minutes, until charred on all sides.
4. When cooking is complete, place the broccoli on a large serving platter. Garnish with red pepper flakes and sesame seeds. Serve immediately.

Blistered Lemony Green Beans

Servings: 4
Cooking Time: 10 Minutes
Ingredients:

- 1 pound haricots verts or green beans, trimmed
- 2 tablespoons vegetable oil
- Juice of 1 lemon
- Pinch red pepper flakes
- Flaky sea salt, to taste
- Freshly ground black pepper, to taste

Directions:

1. Insert the Grill Grate and close the hood. Select GRILL, set the temperature to MAX, and set the time to 10 minutes. Select START/STOP to begin preheating.
2. While the unit is preheating, in a medium bowl, toss the green beans in oil until evenly coated.
3. When the unit beeps to signify it has preheated, place the green beans on the Grill Grate. Close the hood and GRILL for 8 to 10 minutes, tossing frequently until blistered on all sides.
4. When cooking is complete, place the green beans on a large serving platter. Squeeze lemon juice over the green beans, top with red pepper flakes, and season with sea salt and black pepper.

Garlic Fries

Servings: 4
Cooking Time: 20 Minutes
Ingredients:

- 2 large Idaho or russet potatoes (1½ to 2 pounds)
- 1 head garlic (10 to 12 cloves)
- 4 tablespoons avocado oil, divided
- 1 teaspoon sea salt
- Chopped fresh parsley, for garnish

Directions:

1. Cut the potatoes into ¼-inch-thick slices. Place the slices in a large bowl and cover with cold water. Set aside for 30 minutes. This will ensure the potatoes cook well and crisp up perfectly. While the potatoes are soaking, mince the garlic cloves.
2. Drain the potatoes and pat dry using paper towels. In a large bowl, toss the potato slices with 2 tablespoons of avocado oil.
3. Insert the Cooking Pot and Crisper Basket and close the hood. Select AIR CRISP, set the temperature to 390°F, and set the time to 20 minutes. Select START/STOP to begin preheating.
4. While the unit is preheating, in a small bowl, combine the remaining 2 tablespoons of avocado oil with the minced garlic.
5. When the unit beeps to signify it has preheated, put the fries in the Crisper Basket. Close the hood and cook for 10 minutes.
6. After 10 minutes, open the hood and give the basket a shake to toss the fries. Close the hood and continue cooking for 5 minutes. Open the hood again and give the basket a shake. Close the hood and cook for 5 minutes more.
7. When cooking is complete, the fries will be crispy and golden brown. If you like them extra-crispy, continue cooking to your liking. Transfer the fries to a large bowl and drizzle with the garlic oil. Toss and season with the salt. Garnish with the parsley and serve.

Crispy Cod Fingers

Servings: 4
Cooking Time: 12 Minutes
Ingredients:

- 2 eggs
- 2 tablespoons milk
- 2 cups flour
- 1 cup cornmeal
- 1 teaspoon seafood seasoning
- Salt and black pepper, to taste
- 1 cup bread crumbs
- 1 pound cod fillets, cut into 1-inch strips

Directions:

1. Insert the Crisper Basket and close the hood. Select AIR CRISP, set the temperature to 400°F, and set the time to 12 minutes. Select START/STOP to begin preheating.
2. Beat the eggs with the milk in a shallow bowl. In another shallow bowl, combine the flour, cornmeal, seafood seasoning, salt, and pepper. On a plate, place the bread crumbs.
3. Dredge the cod strips, one at a time, in the flour mixture, then in the egg mixture, finally in the bread crumb to coat evenly.
4. Arrange the cod strips in the Crisper Basket. Close the hood and AIR CRISP for 12 minutes until crispy.
5. Transfer the cod strips to a paper towel-lined plate and serve warm.

Blt With Grilled Heirloom Tomato

Servings: 4
Cooking Time: 10 Minutes
Ingredients:

- 8 slices white bread
- 8 tablespoons mayonnaise
- 2 heirloom tomatoes, sliced ¼-inch thick
- 2 tablespoons canola oil
- Sea salt, to taste
- Freshly ground black pepper, to taste
- 8 slices bacon, cooked
- 8 leaves iceberg lettuce

Directions:
1. Insert the Grill Grate, and close the hood. Select GRILL, set the temperature to MAX, and set the time to 10 minutes. Select START/STOP to begin preheating.
2. While the unit is preheating, spread a thin layer of mayonnaise on one side of each piece of bread.
3. When the unit beeps to signify it has preheated, place the bread, mayonnaise-side down, on the Grill Grate. Close the hood and GRILL for 2 to 3 minutes, until crisp.
4. Meanwhile, remove the watery pulp and seeds from the tomato slices. Brush both sides of the tomatoes with the oil and season with salt and pepper.
5. After 2 to 3 minutes, remove the bread and place the tomatoes on the grill. Close the hood and continue grilling for the remaining 6 to 8 minutes.
6. To assemble, spread a thin layer of mayonnaise on the non-grilled sides of the bread. Layer the tomatoes, bacon, and lettuce on the bread, and top with the remaining slices of bread. Slice each sandwich in half and serve.

Cheesy Garlic Bread

Servings: 4
Cooking Time: 8 Minutes
Ingredients:

- 1 loaf (about 1 pound) French bread
- 8 tablespoons (1 stick) unsalted butter, at room temperature
- 1 tablespoon minced garlic
- 1 teaspoon garlic powder
- 1½ cups shredded mozzarella cheese
- ½ cup shredded Colby Jack cheese
- 1 teaspoon dried parsley

Directions:
1. Insert the Grill Grate and close the hood. Select GRILL, set the temperature to MED, and set the time to 8 minutes. Select START/STOP to begin preheating.
2. While the unit is preheating, cut the French bread in half lengthwise. In a small bowl, mix together the butter, garlic, and garlic powder until well combined. Spread the garlic butter on both bread halves. Top each half with the mozzarella and Colby Jack cheeses. Sprinkle the dried parsley on top.
3. When the unit beeps to signify it has preheated, place the cheese-topped bread on the Grill Grate. Close the hood and grill for 8 minutes.
4. When cooking is complete, the cheese will be melted and golden brown. Remove the bread from the grill and serve.

Sweet Potato Chips

Servings:1
Cooking Time: 8 To 10 Hours
Ingredients:

- 1 sweet potato, peeled
- ½ tablespoon avocado oil
- ½ teaspoon sea salt

Directions:
1. Using a mandoline, thinly slice (⅛ inch or less) the sweet potato.
2. In a large bowl, toss the sweet potato slices with the oil until evenly coated. Season with the salt.
3. Place the sweet potato slices flat on the Crisper Basket. Arrange them in a single layer, without any slices touching each another.
4. Place the basket in the pot and close the hood.
5. Select DEHYDRATE, set the temperature to 120ºF, and set the time to 10 hours. Select START/STOP.
6. After 8 hours, check for desired doneness. Continue dehydrating for 2 more hours, if necessary.
7. When cooking is complete, remove the basket from the pot. Transfer the sweet potato chips to an airtight container and store at room temperature.

Breaded Artichoke Hearts

Servings: 14
Cooking Time: 8 Minutes
Ingredients:

- 14 whole artichoke hearts, packed in water
- 1 egg
- ½ cup all-purpose flour
- ⅓ cup panko bread crumbs
- 1 teaspoon Italian seasoning
- Cooking spray

Directions:

1. Insert the Crisper Basket and close the hood. Select AIR CRISP, set the temperature to 380ºF, and set the time to 8 minutes. Select START/STOP to begin preheating.
2. Squeeze excess water from the artichoke hearts and place them on paper towels to dry.
3. In a small bowl, beat the egg. In another small bowl, place the flour. In a third small bowl, combine the bread crumbs and Italian seasoning, and stir.
4. Spritz the Crisper Basket with cooking spray.
5. Dip the artichoke hearts in the flour, then the egg, and then the bread crumb mixture.
6. Place the breaded artichoke hearts in the Crisper Basket. Spray them with cooking spray.
7. Close the hood and AIR CRISP for 8 minutes, or until the artichoke hearts have browned and are crisp, flipping once halfway through.
8. Let cool for 5 minutes before serving.

Caramelized Peaches

Servings: 4
Cooking Time: 10 To 13 Minutes
Ingredients:

- 2 tablespoons sugar
- ¼ teaspoon ground cinnamon
- 4 peaches, cut into wedges
- Cooking spray

Directions:

1. Lightly spray the Crisper Basket with cooking spray.
2. Insert the Crisper Basket and close the hood. Select AIR CRISP, set the temperature to 350ºF, and set the time to 13 minutes. Select START/STOP to begin preheating.
3. Toss the peaches with the sugar and cinnamon in a medium bowl until evenly coated.
4. Arrange the peaches in the Crisper Basket in a single layer. Lightly mist the peaches with cooking spray. You may need to work in batches to avoid overcrowding.
5. Close the hood and AIR CRISP for 5 minutes. Flip the peaches and AIR CRISP for another 5 to 8 minutes, or until the peaches are caramelized.
6. Repeat with the remaining peaches.
7. Let the peaches cool for 5 minutes and serve warm.

Garlicky And Lemony Artichokes

Servings: 4
Cooking Time: 10 Minutes
Ingredients:
- Juice of ½ lemon
- ½ cup canola oil
- 3 garlic cloves, chopped
- Sea salt, to taste
- Freshly ground black pepper, to taste
- 2 large artichokes, trimmed and halved

Directions:
1.   Insert the Grill Grate and close the hood. Select GRILL, set the temperature to MAX, and set the time to 10 minutes. Select START/STOP to begin preheating.
2.   While the unit is preheating, in a medium bowl, combine the lemon juice, oil, and garlic. Season with salt and pepper, then brush the artichoke halves with the lemon-garlic mixture.
3.   When the unit beeps to signify it has preheated, place the artichokes on the Grill Grate, cut side down. Gently press them down to maximize grill marks. Close the hood and GRILL for 8 to 10 minutes, occasionally basting generously with the lemon-garlic mixture throughout cooking, until blistered on all sides.

Easy Muffuletta Sliders With Olives

Servings:8
Cooking Time: 5 To 7 Minutes
Ingredients:
- ¼ pound thinly sliced deli ham
- ¼ pound thinly sliced pastrami
- 4 ounces low-fat Mozzarella cheese, grated
- 8 slider buns, split in half
- Cooking spray
- 1 tablespoon sesame seeds
- Olive Mix:
- ½ cup sliced green olives with pimentos
- ¼ cup sliced black olives
- ¼ cup chopped kalamata olives
- 1 teaspoon red wine vinegar
- ¼ teaspoon basil
- ⅛ teaspoon garlic powder

Directions:
1.   Insert the Crisper Basket and close the hood. Select BAKE, set the temperature to 360ºF, and set the time to 7 minutes. Select START/STOP to begin preheating.
2.   Combine all the ingredients for the olive mix in a small bowl and stir well.
3.   Stir together the ham, pastrami, and cheese in a medium bowl and divide the mixture into 8 equal portions.
4.   Assemble the sliders: Top each bottom bun with 1 portion of meat and cheese, 2 tablespoons of olive mix, finished by the remaining buns. Lightly spritz the tops with cooking spray. Scatter the sesame seeds on top.
5.   Working in batches, arrange the sliders in the Crisper Basket. Close the hood and BAKE for 5 t0 7 minutes until the cheese melts.
6.   Transfer to a large plate and repeat with the remaining sliders.
7.   Serve immediately.

Grilled Blooming Onion

Servings: 4
Cooking Time: 12 Minutes
Ingredients:
- 2 large yellow onions
- 1 cup milk
- 2 large eggs
- 1 teaspoon paprika
- 1 teaspoon cayenne pepper
- 1 teaspoon garlic powder
- 1 teaspoon onion powder
- 2 cups all-purpose flour
- Salt
- Freshly ground black pepper
- Nonstick cooking spray

Directions:

1. Insert the Grill Grate and close the hood. Select GRILL, set the temperature to LO, and set the time to 12 minutes. Select START/STOP to begin preheating.

2. While the unit is preheating, cut off both ends of the onions, keeping the root end as intact as possible. Peel off the outer layer of skin. With the root facing up, begin cutting your petals Starting from ¼ inch below the root end (do not cut through the root), cut downward to slit the onion into 4 equal sections, and then again in between each cut so there are 8 equal sections, and then again to make 16 petals. Turn the onion upside down so the root is now on the bottom, and the petals should begin to open.

3. In a large bowl, whisk together the milk and eggs. Carefully place the blooming onion in the mixture to soak.

4. In a separate large bowl, combine the paprika, cayenne pepper, garlic powder, onion powder, and flour. Season with salt and pepper. Transfer the blooming onion to the bowl with the seasonings. Using your hands, carefully sift some of the mixture into the cracks of the onion, making sure the petals are coated well. Shake off any excess.

5. When the unit beeps to signify it has preheated, generously spray the onion with cooking spray and place it, petals facing up, on the Grill Grate. Close the hood and grill for 10 minutes.

6. After 10 minutes, open the hood and check for crispiness and if the onion is browned to your liking. To continue cooking, generously spray the onion with more cooking spray. Close the hood and continue cooking for 2 minutes more, or until the onions have browned and crisped up to your desired doneness. Remove the onion from the grill and serve.

Bacon-wrapped Dates

Servings: 6
Cooking Time: 10 To 14 Minutes
Ingredients:
- 12 dates, pitted
- 6 slices high-quality bacon, cut in half
- Cooking spray

Directions:

1. Insert the Crisper Basket and close the hood. Select BAKE, set the temperature to 360ºF, and set the time to 7 minutes. Select START/STOP to begin preheating.

2. Wrap each date with half a bacon slice and secure with a toothpick.

3. Spray the Crisper Basket with cooking spray, then place 6 bacon-wrapped dates in the basket. Place the pan directly in the pot. Close the hood and BAKE for 5 to 7 minutes or until the bacon is crispy. Repeat this process with the remaining dates.

4. Remove the dates and allow to cool on a wire rack for 5 minutes before serving.

Sausage And Mushroom Empanadas

Servings: 4
Cooking Time: 12 Minutes
Ingredients:
- ½ pound Kielbasa smoked sausage, chopped
- 4 chopped canned mushrooms
- 2 tablespoons chopped onion
- ½ teaspoon ground cumin
- ¼ teaspoon paprika
- Salt and black pepper, to taste
- ½ package puff pastry dough, at room temperature
- 1 egg, beaten
- Cooking spray

Directions:
1. Spritz the Crisper Basket with cooking spray.
2. Insert the Crisper Basket and close the hood. Select AIR CRISP, set the temperature to 360ºF, and set the time to 12 minutes. Select START/STOP to begin preheating.
3. Combine the sausage, mushrooms, onion, cumin, paprika, salt, and pepper in a bowl and stir to mix well.
4. Make the empanadas: Place the puff pastry dough on a lightly floured surface. Cut circles into the dough with a glass. Place 1 tablespoon of the sausage mixture into the center of each pastry circle. Fold each in half and pinch the edges to seal. Using a fork, crimp the edges. Brush them with the beaten egg and mist with cooking spray.
5. Place the empanadas in the Crisper Basket. Close the hood and AIR CRISP for 12 minutes until golden brown. Flip the empanadas halfway through the cooking time.
6. Allow them to cool for 5 minutes and serve hot.

Buttermilk Marinated Chicken Wings

Servings: 4
Cooking Time: 17 To 19 Minutes
Ingredients:
- 2 pounds chicken wings
- Marinade:
- 1 cup buttermilk
- ½ teaspoon salt
- ½ teaspoon black pepper
- Coating:
- 1 cup flour
- 1 cup panko bread crumbs
- 2 tablespoons poultry seasoning
- 2 teaspoons salt
- Cooking spray

Directions:
1. Whisk together all the ingredients for the marinade in a large bowl.
2. Add the chicken wings to the marinade and toss well. Transfer to the refrigerator to marinate for at least an hour.
3. Spritz the Crisper Basket with cooking spray.
4. Insert the Crisper Basket and close the hood. Select AIR CRISP, set the temperature to 360ºF, and set the time to 19 minutes. Select START/STOP to begin preheating.
5. Thoroughly combine all the ingredients for the coating in a shallow bowl.
6. Remove the chicken wings from the marinade and shake off any excess. Roll them in the coating mixture.
7. Place the chicken wings in the Crisper Basket in a single layer. Mist the wings with cooking spray. You'll need to work in batches to avoid overcrowding.
8. Close the hood and AIR CRISP for 17 to 19 minutes, or until the wings are crisp and golden brown on the outside. Flip the wings halfway through the cooking time.
9. Remove from the basket to a plate and repeat with the remaining wings.
10. Serve hot.

Cayenne Sesame Nut Mix

Servings:4
Cooking Time: 2 Minutes

Ingredients:

- 1 tablespoon buttery spread, melted
- 2 teaspoons honey
- ¼ teaspoon cayenne pepper
- 2 teaspoons sesame seeds
- ¼ teaspoon kosher salt
- ¼ teaspoon freshly ground black pepper

- 1 cup cashews
- 1 cup almonds
- 1 cup mini pretzels
- 1 cup rice squares cereal
- Cooking spray

Directions:

1. Select BAKE, set the temperature to 360ºF, and set the time to 2 minutes. Select START/STOP to begin preheating.
2. In a large bowl, combine the buttery spread, honey, cayenne pepper, sesame seeds, kosher salt, and black pepper, then add the cashews, almonds, pretzels, and rice squares, tossing to coat.
3. Spray a baking pan with cooking spray, then pour the mixture into the pan. Place the pan directly in the pot. Close the hood and BAKE for 2 minutes.
4. Remove the sesame mix from the grill and allow to cool in the pan on a wire rack for 5 minutes before serving.

Cuban Sandwiches

Servings:4
Cooking Time: 8 Minutes

Ingredients:

- 8 slices ciabatta bread, about ¼-inch thick
- Cooking spray
- 1 tablespoon brown mustard
- Toppings:

- 6 to 8 ounces thinly sliced leftover roast pork
- 4 ounces thinly sliced deli turkey
- ⅓ cup bread and butter pickle slices
- 2 to 3 ounces Pepper Jack cheese slices

Directions:

1. Insert the Crisper Basket and close the hood. Select AIR CRISP, set the temperature to 390ºF, and set the time to 8 minutes. Select START/STOP to begin preheating.
2. On a clean work surface, spray one side of each slice of bread with cooking spray. Spread the other side of each slice of bread evenly with brown mustard.
3. Top 4 of the bread slices with the roast pork, turkey, pickle slices, cheese, and finish with remaining bread slices. Transfer to the Crisper Basket.
4. Close the hood and AIR CRISP for 8 minutes until golden brown.
5. Cool for 5 minutes and serve warm.

Spicy Kale Chips

Servings: 4
Cooking Time: 8 To 12 Minutes

Ingredients:

- 5 cups kale, large stems removed and chopped
- 2 teaspoons canola oil
- ¼ teaspoon smoked paprika
- ¼ teaspoon kosher salt
- Cooking spray

Directions:

1. Insert the Crisper Basket and close the hood. Select AIR CRISP, set the temperature to 390ºF, and set the time to 6 minutes. Select START/STOP to begin preheating.
2. In a large bowl, toss the kale, canola oil, smoked paprika, and kosher salt.
3. Spray the Crisper Basket with cooking spray, then place half the kale in the basket. Close the hood and AIR CRISP for 2 to 3 minutes.
4. Shake the basket and AIR CRISP for 2 to 3 more minutes, or until crispy. Repeat this process with the remaining kale.
5. Remove the kale and allow to cool on a wire rack for 3 to 5 minutes before serving.

Grilled Carrots With Honey Glazed

Servings: 4
Cooking Time: 10 Minutes
Ingredients:

- 6 medium carrots, peeled and cut lengthwise
- 1 tablespoon canola oil
- 2 tablespoons unsalted butter, melted
- ¼ cup brown sugar, melted
- ¼ cup honey
- ⅛ teaspoon sea salt

Directions:

1. Insert the Grill Grate and close the hood. Select GRILL, set the temperature to MAX, and set the time to 10 minutes. Select START/STOP to begin preheating.
2. In a large bowl, toss the carrots and oil until well coated.
3. When the unit beeps to signify it has preheated, place carrots on the center of the Grill Grate. Close the hood and GRILL for 5 minutes.
4. Meanwhile, in a small bowl, whisk together the butter, brown sugar, honey, and salt.
5. After 5 minutes, open the hood and baste the carrots with the glaze. Using tongs, turn the carrots and baste the other side. Close the hood and GRILL for another 5 minutes.
6. When cooking is complete, serve immediately.

Mushroom And Spinach Calzones

Servings: 4
Cooking Time: 26 To 27 Minutes
Ingredients:

- 2 tablespoons olive oil
- 1 onion, chopped
- 2 garlic cloves, minced
- ¼ cup chopped mushrooms
- 1 pound spinach, chopped
- 1 tablespoon Italian seasoning
- ½ teaspoon oregano
- Salt and black pepper, to taste
- 1½ cups marinara sauce
- 1 cup ricotta cheese, crumbled
- 1 pizza crust
- Cooking spray

Directions:

1. Make the Filling:
2. Heat the olive oil in a pan over medium heat until shimmering.
3. Add the onion, garlic, and mushrooms and sauté for 4 minutes, or until softened.
4. Stir in the spinach and sauté for 2 to 3 minutes, or until the spinach is wilted. Sprinkle with the Italian seasoning, oregano, salt, and pepper and mix well.
5. Add the marinara sauce and cook for about 5 minutes, stirring occasionally, or until the sauce is thickened.
6. Remove the pan from the heat and stir in the ricotta cheese. Set aside.
7. Make the Calzones:
8. Spritz the Crisper Basket with cooking spray.
9. Insert the Crisper Basket and close the hood. Select AIR CRISP, set the temperature to 375°F, and set the time to 15 minutes. Select START/STOP to begin preheating.
10. Roll the pizza crust out with a rolling pin on a lightly floured work surface, then cut it into 4 rectangles.
11. Spoon ¼ of the filling into each rectangle and fold in half. Crimp the edges with a fork to seal. Mist them with cooking spray.
12. Place the calzones in the Crisper Basket. Close the hood and AIR CRISP for 15 minutes, flipping once, or until the calzones are golden brown and crisp.
13. Transfer the calzones to a paper towel-lined plate and serve.

Poultry

Spiced Breaded Chicken Cutlets

Servings: 2
Cooking Time: 11 Minutes
Ingredients:
- ½ pound boneless, skinless chicken breasts, horizontally sliced in half, into cutlets
- ½ tablespoon extra-virgin olive oil
- ⅛ cup bread crumbs
- ¼ teaspoon sea salt
- ¼ teaspoon freshly ground black pepper
- ¼ teaspoon paprika
- ¼ teaspoon garlic powder
- ⅛ teaspoon onion powder

Directions:
1. Insert the Crisper Basket and close the hood. Select AIR CRISP, set the temperature to 375ºF, and set the time to 11 minutes. Select START/STOP to begin preheating.
2. Brush each side of the chicken cutlets with the oil.
3. Combine the bread crumbs, salt, pepper, paprika, garlic powder, and onion powder in a medium shallow bowl. Dredge the chicken cutlets in the bread crumb mixture, turning several times, to ensure the chicken is fully coated.
4. When the unit beeps to signify it has preheated, place the chicken in the basket. Close the hood and AIR CRISP for 9 minutes. Cooking is complete when the internal temperature of the meat reaches at least 165ºF on a food thermometer. If needed, AIR CRISP for up to 2 minutes more.
5. Remove the chicken cutlets and serve immediately.

Blackened Chicken

Servings: 4
Cooking Time: 10 Minutes
Ingredients:
- 1 tablespoon paprika
- 1 tablespoon garlic powder
- 1 tablespoon onion powder
- 1 tablespoon freshly ground black pepper
- 1 teaspoon Italian seasoning
- 1 teaspoon salt
- ½ teaspoon ground cumin
- ½ teaspoon cayenne pepper
- 4 tablespoons (½ stick) unsalted butter, melted
- ¼ cup avocado oil
- 4 boneless, skinless chicken breasts (about 2 pounds), halved crosswise

Directions:
1. Insert the Grill Grate and close the hood. Select GRILL, set the temperature to HI, and set the time to 10 minutes. Select START/STOP to begin preheating.
2. In a small bowl, combine the paprika, garlic powder, onion powder, black pepper, Italian seasoning, salt, cumin, and cayenne pepper.
3. In a separate small bowl, whisk together the butter and avocado oil. Lightly coat the chicken breasts on both sides with the butter-and-oil mixture, and then season both sides with the spice mix to get a nice coating.
4. When the unit beeps to signify it has preheated, open the hood and place the seasoned chicken on the Grill Grate. Close the hood and grill for 5 minutes.
5. After 5 minutes, open the hood and flip the chicken. Close the hood and cook for 5 minutes more.
6. When cooking is complete, remove the chicken from the grill and serve.

Soy-garlic Crispy Chicken

Servings: 4
Cooking Time: 20 Minutes
Ingredients:
- 20 to 24 chicken wings
- 2 tablespoons cornstarch
- ¼ cup soy sauce
- ½ cup water
- 1 tablespoon sesame oil
- 1 teaspoon peeled minced fresh ginger
- 1 teaspoon garlic powder
- 1 teaspoon onion powder
- 1 tablespoon oyster sauce
- 2 tablespoons honey
- 1 tablespoon rice vinegar
- 1 tablespoon light brown sugar, packed

Directions:
1. Insert the Grill Grate and close the hood. Select GRILL, set the temperature to MED, and set the time to 20 minutes. Select START/STOP to begin preheating.
2. While the unit is preheating, pat the chicken wings dry with a paper towel and place them in a large bowl. Sprinkle the wings with the cornstarch and toss to coat.
3. In a separate large bowl, whisk together the soy sauce, water, sesame oil, ginger, garlic powder, onion powder, oyster sauce, honey, rice vinegar, and brown sugar until the sugar is dissolved. Place half the sauce in a small bowl and set aside.
4. When the unit beeps to signify it has preheated, place the chicken wings on the Grill Grate. Close the hood and cook for 10 minutes.
5. After 10 minutes, open the hood and flip the wings. Using a basting brush, brush the soy-garlic sauce from the small bowl on the chicken wings. Close the hood and cook for 10 minutes more.
6. When cooking is complete, remove the wings from the grill and place in the large bowl with the remaining soy-garlic sauce. Toss and coat the wings with the sauce, then serve.

Sriracha-honey Glazed Chicken Thighs

Servings: 4
Cooking Time: 17 Minutes
Ingredients:
- 1 cup sriracha
- Juice of 2 lemons
- ¼ cup honey
- 4 bone-in chicken thighs

Directions:
1. Place the sriracha, lemon juice, and honey in a large resealable plastic bag or container. Add the chicken thighs and toss to coat evenly. Refrigerate for 30 minutes.
2. Insert the Grill Grate and close the hood. Select GRILL, set the temperature to MEDIUM, and set the time to 14 minutes. Select START/STOP to begin preheating.
3. When the unit beeps to signify it has preheated, place the chicken thighs onto the Grill Grate, gently pressing them down to maximize grill marks. Close the hood and GRILL for 7 minutes.
4. After 7 minutes, flip the chicken thighs using tongs. Close the hood and GRILL for 7 minutes more.
5. Cooking is complete when the internal temperature of the meat reaches at least 165ºF on a food thermometer. If necessary, close the hood and continue grilling for 2 to 3 minutes more.
6. When cooking is complete, remove the chicken from the grill, and let it rest for 5 minutes before serving.

Roasted Cajun Turkey

Servings: 4
Cooking Time: 30 Minutes
Ingredients:

- 2 pounds turkey thighs, skinless and boneless
- 1 red onion, sliced
- 2 bell peppers, sliced
- 1 habanero pepper, minced
- 1 carrot, sliced
- 1 tablespoon Cajun seasoning mix
- 1 tablespoon fish sauce
- 2 cups chicken broth
- Nonstick cooking spray

Directions:

1. Select ROAST, set the temperature to 360ºF, and set the time to 30 minutes. Select START/STOP to begin preheating.
2. Spritz the bottom and sides of the pot with nonstick cooking spray.
3. Arrange the turkey thighs in the pot. Add the onion, peppers, and carrot. Sprinkle with Cajun seasoning. Add the fish sauce and chicken broth.
4. Close the hood and ROAST for 30 minutes until cooked through. Serve warm.

Ginger Chicken Thighs

Servings: 4
Cooking Time: 10 Minutes
Ingredients:

- ¼ cup julienned peeled fresh ginger
- 2 tablespoons vegetable oil
- 1 tablespoon honey
- 1 tablespoon soy sauce
- 1 tablespoon ketchup
- 1 teaspoon garam masala
- 1 teaspoon ground turmeric
- ¼ teaspoon kosher salt
- ½ teaspoon cayenne pepper
- Vegetable oil spray
- 1 pound boneless, skinless chicken thighs, cut crosswise into thirds
- ¼ cup chopped fresh cilantro, for garnish

Directions:

1. In a small bowl, combine the ginger, oil, honey, soy sauce, ketchup, garam masala, turmeric, salt, and cayenne. Whisk until well combined. Place the chicken in a resealable plastic bag and pour the marinade over. Seal the bag and massage to cover all of the chicken with the marinade. Marinate at room temperature for 30 minutes or in the refrigerator for up to 24 hours.
2. Insert the Crisper Basket and close the hood. Select BAKE, set the temperature to 350ºF, and set the time to 10 minutes. Select START/STOP to begin preheating.
3. Spray the Crisper Basket with vegetable oil spray and add the chicken and as much of the marinade and julienned ginger as possible.
4. Close the hood and BAKE for 10 minutes. Use a meat thermometer to ensure the chicken has reached an internal temperature of 165ºF.
5. To serve, garnish with cilantro.

Teriyaki Chicken And Bell Pepper Kebabs

Servings: 4
Cooking Time: 14 Minutes

Ingredients:

- 1 pound boneless, skinless chicken breasts, cut into 2-inch cubes
- 1 cup teriyaki sauce, divided
- 2 green bell peppers, seeded and cut into 1-inch cubes
- 2 cups fresh pineapple, cut into 1-inch cubes

Directions:

1. Place the chicken and ½ cup of teriyaki sauce in a large resealable plastic bag or container. Toss to coat evenly. Refrigerate for at least 30 minutes.
2. Insert the Grill Grate and close the hood. Select GRILL, set the temperature to MEDIUM, and set the time to 14 minutes. Select START/STOP to begin preheating.
3. While the unit is preheating, assemble the kebabs by threading the chicken onto the wood skewers, alternating with the peppers and pineapple. Ensure the ingredients are pushed almost completely down to the end of the skewers.
4. When the unit beeps to signify it has preheated, place the skewers on the Grill Grate. Close the hood and GRILL for 10 to 14 minutes, occasionally basting the kebabs with the remaining ½ cup of teriyaki sauce while cooking.
5. Cooking is complete when the internal temperature of the chicken reaches 165ºF on a food thermometer.

Cilantro-lime Chicken Thighs

Servings: 4
Cooking Time: 15 Minutes

Ingredients:

- ½ cup extra-virgin olive oil
- 4 tablespoons light brown sugar, packed
- 4 tablespoons soy sauce
- Juice of 2 key limes
- Zest of 1 key lime
- 2 teaspoons sea salt
- ½ teaspoon freshly ground black pepper
- 2 tablespoons minced garlic
- ½ cup chopped fresh cilantro
- 3 pounds bone-in, skin-on chicken thighs

Directions:

1. In a large bowl, whisk together the olive oil, brown sugar, soy sauce, lime juice, lime zest, salt, pepper, minced garlic, and cilantro. Place the chicken thighs in the marinade and turn so the meat is fully coated. Cover the bowl and refrigerate for at least 1 hour or up to overnight.
2. Insert the Grill Grate and close the hood. Select GRILL, set the temperature to LO, and set the time to 15 minutes. Select START/STOP to begin preheating.
3. When the unit beeps to signify it has preheated, place the chicken thighs skin-side up on the Grill Grate. Brush some of the marinade on the chicken. Close the hood and grill for 8 minutes.
4. After 8 minutes, open the hood and flip the chicken. Close the hood and continue cooking for 7 minutes more.

Turkey And Cauliflower Meatloaf

Servings: 6
Cooking Time: 50 Minutes

Ingredients:

- 2 pounds lean ground turkey
- 1⅓ cups riced cauliflower
- 2 large eggs, lightly beaten
- ¼ cup almond flour
- ⅔ cup chopped yellow or white onion
- 1 teaspoon ground dried turmeric
- 1 teaspoon ground cumin
- 1 teaspoon ground coriander
- 1 tablespoon minced garlic
- 1 teaspoon salt
- 1 teaspoon ground black pepper
- Cooking spray

Directions:

1. Select BAKE, set the temperature to 350ºF, and set the time to 25 minutes. Select START/STOP to begin preheating.
2. Spritz a loaf pan with cooking spray.
3. Combine all the ingredients in a large bowl. Stir to mix well. Pour half of the mixture in the prepared loaf pan and press with a spatula to coat the bottom evenly. Spritz the mixture with cooking spray.
4. Place the pan directly in the pot. Close the hood and BAKE for 25 minutes, or until the meat is well browned and the internal temperature reaches at least 165ºF. Repeat with remaining mixture.
5. Remove the loaf pan from the grill and serve immediately.

Easy Asian Turkey Meatballs

Servings: 4
Cooking Time: 11 To 14 Minutes
Ingredients:

- 2 tablespoons peanut oil, divided
- 1 small onion, minced
- ¼ cup water chestnuts, finely chopped
- ½ teaspoon ground ginger
- 2 tablespoons low-sodium soy sauce
- ¼ cup panko bread crumbs
- 1 egg, beaten
- 1 pound ground turkey

Directions:

1. Select AIR CRISP, set the temperature to 400°F, and set the time to 2 minutes. Select START/STOP to begin preheating.
2. In a round metal pan, combine 1 tablespoon of peanut oil and onion. Place the pan directly in the pot. Close the hood and AIR CRISP for 1 to 2 minutes or until crisp and tender. Transfer the onion to a medium bowl.
3. Add the water chestnuts, ground ginger, soy sauce, and bread crumbs to the onion and mix well. Add egg and stir well. Mix in the ground turkey until combined.
4. Form the mixture into 1-inch meatballs. Drizzle the remaining 1 tablespoon of oil over the meatballs. Arrange the meatballs in the pan.
5. Place the pan directly in the pot. Close the hood and BAKE for 10 to 12 minutes, or until they are 165°F on a meat thermometer. Rest for 5 minutes before serving.

Lemon And Rosemary Chicken

Servings: 4
Cooking Time: 15 Minutes
Ingredients:

- 3 pounds bone-in, skin-on chicken thighs
- 4 tablespoons avocado oil
- 2 tablespoons lemon-pepper seasoning
- 1 tablespoon chopped fresh rosemary
- 1 lemon, thinly sliced

Directions:

1. Insert the Grill Grate and close the hood. Select GRILL, set the temperature to LO, and set the time to 15 minutes. Select START/STOP to begin preheating.
2. Coat the chicken thighs with the avocado oil and rub the lemon-pepper seasoning and rosemary evenly over the chicken.
3. When the unit beeps to signify it has preheated, place the chicken thighs on the Grill Grate, skin-side up. Place the lemon slices on top of the chicken. Close the hood and grill for 8 minutes.
4. After 8 minutes, open the hood and remove the lemon slices. Flip the chicken and place the lemon slices back on top. Close the hood and cook for 7 minutes more.
5. When cooking is complete, remove the chicken from the grill and serve.

Adobo Chicken

Servings: 4
Cooking Time: 15 Minutes
Ingredients:
- 2 tablespoons soy sauce
- 2 tablespoons rice vinegar
- 1 tablespoon balsamic vinegar
- ¼ teaspoon freshly ground black pepper
- 4 garlic cloves, minced
- ½ teaspoon peeled minced fresh ginger
- Juice of ½ lemon
- ¼ teaspoon granulated sugar
- 3 bay leaves
- Pinch Italian seasoning (optional)
- Pinch ground cumin (optional)
- 3 pounds chicken drumsticks

Directions:
1. In a large bowl, whisk together the soy sauce, rice vinegar, balsamic vinegar, pepper, garlic, ginger, lemon juice, sugar, bay leaves, Italian seasoning (if using), and cumin (if using). Add the drumsticks to the marinade, making sure the meat is coated. Cover and refrigerate for at least 1 hour. If you have the time, marinate the chicken overnight to let all the flavors settle in.
2. Insert the Grill Grate and close the hood. Select GRILL, set the temperature to MED, and set the time to 15 minutes. Select START/STOP to begin preheating.
3. When the unit beeps to signify it has preheated, place the chicken drumsticks on the Grill Grate. Brush any leftover marinade onto the drumsticks. Close the hood and grill for 8 minutes.
4. After 8 minutes, open the hood and flip the drumsticks. Close the hood and continue cooking for 7 minutes more.
5. When cooking is complete, remove the drumsticks from the grill and serve.

Crispy Chicken Parmigiana

Servings: 4
Cooking Time: 15 Minutes
Ingredients:
- 2 large eggs
- 2 cups panko bread crumbs
- ½ cup shredded Parmesan cheese
- 1 tablespoon Italian seasoning
- 1 teaspoon garlic powder
- 1½ pounds boneless, skinless chicken breasts (about 3 breasts), halved lengthwise
- 3 cups marinara sauce, hot
- ½ cup grated Parmesan cheese

Directions:
1. Insert the Grill Grate and close the hood. Select GRILL, set the temperature to MED, and set the time to 15 minutes. Select START/STOP to begin preheating.
2. While the unit is preheating, create an assembly line with 2 large bowls. In one bowl, whisk the eggs. In the other bowl, combine the panko bread crumbs, shredded Parmesan cheese, Italian seasoning, and garlic powder. Dip each chicken breast in the egg and then into the bread crumb mix until fully coated. Set the coated chicken on a plate or tray.
3. When the unit beeps to signify it has preheated, place the chicken on the Grill Grate. Close the hood and grill for 8 minutes.
4. After 8 minutes, open the hood and flip the chicken. Close the hood and continue cooking for 7 minutes more.
5. When cooking is complete, remove the chicken from the grill and top with the marinara sauce and grated Parmesan cheese.

Turkey Stuffed Bell Peppers

Servings: 4
Cooking Time: 15 Minutes
Ingredients:

- ½ pound lean ground turkey
- 4 medium bell peppers
- 1 can black beans, drained and rinsed
- 1 cup shredded reduced-fat Cheddar cheese
- 1 cup cooked long-grain brown rice
- 1 cup mild salsa
- 1¼ teaspoons chili powder
- 1 teaspoon salt
- ½ teaspoon ground cumin
- ½ teaspoon freshly ground black pepper
- Olive oil spray
- Chopped fresh cilantro, for garnish

Directions:
1. Insert the Crisper Basket and close the hood. Select AIR CRISP, set the temperature to 360ºF, and set the time to 15 minutes. Select START/STOP to begin preheating.
2. In a large skillet over medium-high heat, cook the turkey, breaking it up with a spoon, until browned, about 5 minutes. Drain off any excess fat.
3. Cut about ½ inch off the tops of the peppers and then cut in half lengthwise. Remove and discard the seeds and set the peppers aside.
4. In a large bowl, combine the browned turkey, black beans, Cheddar cheese, rice, salsa, chili powder, salt, cumin, and black pepper. Spoon the mixture into the bell peppers.
5. Lightly spray the Crisper Basket with olive oil spray.
6. Place the stuffed peppers in the Crisper Basket. Close the hood and AIR CRISP for 10 to 15 minutes until heated through.
7. Garnish with cilantro and serve.

Garlic Brown-butter Chicken With Tomatoes

Servings: 4
Cooking Time: 15 Minutes
Ingredients:

- 4 boneless, skinless chicken breasts
- Extra-virgin olive oil
- ½ teaspoon paprika
- ½ teaspoon sea salt
- 12 tablespoons (1½ sticks) unsalted butter
- 4 garlic cloves, minced
- 2 tablespoons light brown sugar, packed
- ½ teaspoon garlic powder
- 6 ounces cherry tomatoes

Directions:
1. Insert the Cooking Pot and close the hood. Select GRILL, set the temperature to MED, and set the time to 15 minutes. Select START/STOP to begin preheating.
2. While the unit is preheating, drizzle the chicken breasts with olive oil, then lightly sprinkle both sides with the paprika and salt.
3. When the unit beeps to signify it has preheated, place the butter and garlic in the Cooking Pot. Insert the Grill Grate on top and place the chicken breasts on the Grill Grate. Close the hood and grill for 8 minutes.
4. After 8 minutes, open the hood and use grill mitts to remove the Grill Grate and chicken. Add the brown sugar, garlic powder, and tomatoes to the butter and garlic and stir.
5. Transfer the chicken to the Cooking Pot, making sure you flip the breasts. Coat the chicken with the brown butter sauce. Close the hood and cook for 7 minutes more.
6. When cooking is complete, remove the chicken and place on a plate. Spoon the sauce over and serve.

Buttermilk Ranch Chicken Tenders

Servings: 4
Cooking Time: 10 Minutes
Ingredients:

- 2 cups buttermilk
- 1 (0.4-ounce) packet ranch seasoning mix
- 1½ pounds boneless, skinless chicken breasts (about 3 breasts), cut into 1-inch strips
- 2 cups all-purpose flour
- ¼ teaspoon paprika
- ¼ teaspoon garlic powder
- ¼ teaspoon baking powder
- 2 teaspoons salt
- 2 large eggs
- ¼ cup avocado oil, divided

Directions:

1. In a large bowl, whisk together the buttermilk and ranch seasoning. Place the chicken strips in the bowl. Cover and let marinate in the refrigerator for 30 minutes.
2. Create an assembly line with 2 large bowls. Combine the flour, paprika, garlic powder, baking powder, and salt in one bowl. In the other bowl, whisk together the eggs. One at a time, remove the chicken strips from the marinade, shaking off any excess liquid. Dredge the chicken strip in the seasoned flour, coating both sides, then dip it in the beaten egg. Finally, dip it back into the seasoned flour bowl again. Shake any excess flour off. Repeat the process with all the chicken strips, setting them aside on a flat tray or plate once coated.
3. Insert the Grill Grate and close the hood. Select GRILL, set the temperature to MED, and set the time to 10 minutes. Select START/STOP to begin preheating.
4. While the unit is preheating, use a basting brush to generously coat one side of the chicken strips with half of the avocado oil.
5. When the unit beeps to signify it has preheated, place the chicken strips on the grill, oiled-side down. Brush the top of the chicken strips with the rest of the avocado oil. Close the hood and grill for 5 minutes.
6. After 5 minutes, open the hood and flip the chicken strips. Close the hood and continue cooking for 5 minutes more.
7. When cooking is complete, the chicken strips will be golden brown and crispy. Remove them from the grill and serve.

Maple-teriyaki Chicken Wings

Servings: 4
Cooking Time: 14 Minutes
Ingredients:

- 1 cup maple syrup
- ⅓ cup soy sauce
- ¼ cup teriyaki sauce
- 3 garlic cloves, minced
- 2 teaspoons garlic powder
- 2 teaspoons onion powder
- 1 teaspoon freshly ground black pepper
- 2 pounds bone-in chicken wings (drumettes and flats)

Directions:

1. Insert the Grill Grate and close the hood. Select GRILL, set the temperature to MEDIUM, and set the time to 14 minutes. Select START/STOP to begin preheating.
2. Meanwhile, in a large bowl, whisk together the maple syrup, soy sauce, teriyaki sauce, garlic, garlic powder, onion powder, and black pepper. Add the wings, and use tongs to toss and coat.
3. When the unit has beeped to signify it has preheated, place the chicken wings on the Grill Grate. Close the hood and GRILL for 5 minutes. After 5 minutes, flip the wings, close the hood, and GRILL for an additional 5 minutes.
4. Check the wings for doneness. Cooking is complete when the internal temperature of the meat reaches at least 165°F on a food thermometer. If needed, GRILL for up to 4 minutes more.
5. Remove from the grill and serve.

Chicken Cordon Bleu Roll-ups

Servings: 4
Cooking Time: 15 Minutes
Ingredients:
- 1 tablespoon garlic powder
- 1 tablespoon onion powder
- 1½ pounds boneless, skinless chicken breasts (about 3 breasts)
- 6 ounces thin-sliced deli ham
- 6 ounces Swiss cheese, sliced
- 2 large eggs
- 1 cup plain bread crumbs
- ¼ cup sour cream
- 3 tablespoons Dijon mustard
- ¼ teaspoon granulated sugar or honey

Directions:
1. Insert the Grill Grate and close the hood. Select GRILL, set the temperature to MED, and set the time to 15 minutes. Select START/STOP to begin preheating.
2. In a small bowl, combine the garlic powder and onion powder.
3. Cut each chicken breast in half from the side (parallel to the cutting board) to create 6 thinner, flatter chicken breasts. Lightly coat the chicken all over with the garlic-and-onion mixture.
4. Layer 3 or 4 slices of ham on top of each piece of chicken, and top with about 1 ounce of cheese. Starting at the short end, roll the chicken breasts to wrap the ham and cheese inside. Secure the chicken roll-ups with toothpicks.
5. In a large bowl, whisk the eggs. Put the bread crumbs in a separate large bowl. Dip the chicken roll-ups in the egg and then into the bread crumbs until fully coated.
6. When the unit beeps to signify it has preheated, place the roll-ups on the Grill Grate. Close the hood and grill for 7 minutes, 30 seconds.
7. After 7 minutes, 30 seconds, open the hood and flip the roll-ups. Close the hood and continue cooking for 7 minutes, 30 seconds more.
8. While the roll-ups are cooking, in a small bowl, combine the sour cream, Dijon mustard, and sugar and stir until the sugar is dissolved.
9. When cooking is complete, remove the roll-ups from the grill and serve with the sauce, for dipping.

Sweet-and-sour Drumsticks

Servings: 4
Cooking Time: 23 To 25 Minutes
Ingredients:
- 6 chicken drumsticks
- 3 tablespoons lemon juice, divided
- 3 tablespoons low-sodium soy sauce, divided
- 1 tablespoon peanut oil
- 3 tablespoons honey
- 3 tablespoons brown sugar
- 2 tablespoons ketchup
- ¼ cup pineapple juice

Directions:
1. Insert the Crisper Basket and close the hood. Select BAKE, set the temperature to 350ºF, and set the time to 18 minutes. Select START/STOP to begin preheating.
2. Sprinkle the drumsticks with 1 tablespoon of lemon juice and 1 tablespoon of soy sauce. Place in the Crisper Basket and drizzle with the peanut oil. Toss to coat. Close the hood and BAKE for 18 minutes, or until the chicken is almost done.
3. Meanwhile, in a metal bowl, combine the remaining 2 tablespoons of lemon juice, the remaining 2 tablespoons of soy sauce, honey, brown sugar, ketchup, and pineapple juice.
4. Add the cooked chicken to the bowl and stir to coat the chicken well with the sauce.
5. Place the metal bowl in the basket. Bake for 5 to 7 minutes or until the chicken is glazed and registers 165ºF on a meat thermometer. Serve warm.

Spiced Turkey Tenderloin

Servings: 4
Cooking Time: 30 Minutes
Ingredients:
- ½ teaspoon paprika
- ½ teaspoon garlic powder
- ½ teaspoon salt
- ½ teaspoon freshly ground black pepper
- Pinch cayenne pepper
- 1½ pounds turkey breast tenderloin
- Olive oil spray

Directions:
1. Spray the Crisper Basket lightly with olive oil spray.
2. Insert the Crisper Basket and close the hood. Select AIR CRISP, set the temperature to 370ºF, and set the time to 30 minutes. Select START/STOP to begin preheating.
3. In a small bowl, combine the paprika, garlic powder, salt, black pepper, and cayenne pepper. Rub the mixture all over the turkey.
4. Place the turkey in the Crisper Basket and lightly spray with olive oil spray.
5. Close the hood and AIR CRISP for 15 minutes. Flip the turkey over and lightly spray with olive oil spray. AIR CRISP until the internal temperature reaches at least 170ºF for an additional 10 to 15 minutes.
6. Let the turkey rest for 10 minutes before slicing and serving.

Sweet And Spicy Turkey Meatballs

Servings: 6
Cooking Time: 15 Minutes
Ingredients:
- 1 pound lean ground turkey
- ½ cup whole-wheat panko bread crumbs
- 1 egg, beaten
- 1 tablespoon soy sauce
- ¼ cup plus 1 tablespoon hoisin sauce, divided
- 2 teaspoons minced garlic
- ⅛ teaspoon salt
- ⅛ teaspoon freshly ground black pepper
- 1 teaspoon sriracha
- Olive oil spray

Directions:
1. Spray the Crisper Basket lightly with olive oil spray.
2. Insert the Crisper Basket and close the hood. Select AIR CRISP, set the temperature to 350ºF, and set the time to 15 minutes. Select START/STOP to begin preheating.
3. In a large bowl, mix together the turkey, panko bread crumbs, egg, soy sauce, 1 tablespoon of hoisin sauce, garlic, salt, and black pepper.
4. Using a tablespoon, form the mixture into 24 meatballs.
5. In a small bowl, combine the remaining ¼ cup of hoisin sauce and sriracha to make a glaze and set aside.
6. Place the meatballs in the Crisper Basket in a single layer. You may need to cook them in batches.
7. Close the hood and AIR CRISP for 8 minutes. Brush the meatballs generously with the glaze and AIR CRISP until cooked through, an additional 4 to 7 minutes.
8. Serve warm.

Spicy Bbq Chicken Drumsticks

Servings: 4
Cooking Time: 20 Minutes
Ingredients:

- 2 cups barbecue sauce
- Juice of 1 lime
- 2 tablespoons honey
- 1 tablespoon hot sauce
- Sea salt, to taste
- Freshly ground black pepper, to taste
- 1 pound chicken drumsticks

Directions:

1. In a large bowl, combine the barbecue sauce, lime juice, honey, and hot sauce. Season with salt and pepper. Set aside ½ cup of the sauce. Add the drumsticks to the bowl, and toss until evenly coated.
2. Insert the Grill Grate and close the hood. Select GRILL, set the temperature to MEDIUM, and set the time to 20 minutes. Select START/STOP to begin preheating.
3. When the unit beeps to signify it has preheated, place the drumsticks on the Grill Grate. Close the hood and GRILL for 18 minutes, basting often during cooking.
4. Cooking is complete when the internal temperature of the meat reaches at least 165ºF on a food thermometer. If necessary, close the hood and continue grilling for 2 minutes more.

Herbed Grilled Chicken Thighs

Servings: 4
Cooking Time: 13 Minutes
Ingredients:

- Grated zest of 2 lemons
- Juice of 2 lemons
- 3 sprigs fresh rosemary, leaves finely chopped
- 3 sprigs fresh sage, leaves finely chopped
- 2 garlic cloves, minced
- ¼ teaspoon red pepper flakes
- ¼ cup canola oil
- Sea salt
- 4 boneless chicken thighs

Directions:

1. In a small bowl, whisk together the lemon zest and juice, rosemary, sage, garlic, red pepper flakes, and oil. Season with salt.
2. Place the chicken and lemon-herb mixture in a large resealable plastic bag or container. Toss to coat evenly. Refrigerate the chicken for at least 30 minutes.
3. Insert the Grill Grate and close the hood. Select GRILL, set the temperature to HIGH, and set the time to 13 minutes. Select START/STOP to begin preheating.
4. When the unit beeps to signify it has preheated, place the chicken on the Grill Grate. Close the hood and GRILL for 10 to 13 minutes.
5. Cooking is complete when the internal temperature of the chicken reaches at least 165ºF on a food thermometer.

Hearty Turkey Burger

Servings: 4
Cooking Time: 13 Minutes
Ingredients:
- 1 pound ground turkey
- ½ red onion, minced
- 1 jalapeño pepper, seeded, stemmed, and minced
- 3 tablespoons bread crumbs
- 1½ teaspoons ground cumin
- 1 teaspoon paprika
- ½ teaspoon cayenne pepper
- ½ teaspoon sea salt
- ½ teaspoon freshly ground black pepper
- 4 burger buns, for serving
- Lettuce, tomato, and cheese, if desired, for serving
- Ketchup and mustard, if desired, for serving

Directions:
1. Insert the Grill Grate and close the hood. Select GRILL, set the temperature to HIGH, and set the time to 13 minutes. Select START/STOP to begin preheating.
2. Meanwhile, in a large bowl, use your hands to combine the ground turkey, red onion, jalapeño pepper, bread crumbs, cumin, paprika, cayenne pepper, salt, and black pepper. Mix until just combined; be careful not to overwork the burger mixture.
3. Dampen your hands with cool water and form the turkey mixture into four patties.
4. When the unit beeps to signify it has preheated, place the burgers on the Grill Grate. Close the hood and GRILL for 11 minutes.
5. After 11 minutes, check the burgers for doneness. Cooking is complete when the internal temperature reaches at least 165ºF on a food thermometer. If necessary, close the hood and continue grilling for up to 2 minutes more.
6. Once the burgers are done cooking, place each patty on a bun. Top with your preferred fixings, such as lettuce, tomato, cheese, ketchup, and/or mustard.

Turkey Meatballs With Cranberry Sauce

Servings: 4
Cooking Time: 20 Minutes
Ingredients:
- 2 tablespoons onion powder
- 1 cup plain bread crumbs
- 2 large eggs
- 2 tablespoons light brown sugar, packed
- 1 tablespoon salt
- 2 pounds ground turkey
- 1 (14-ounce) can cranberry sauce

Directions:
1. In a large bowl, mix together the onion powder, bread crumbs, eggs, brown sugar, and salt. Place the ground turkey in the bowl. Using your hands, mix the ingredients together just until combined (overmixing can make the meat tough and chewy). Form the mixture into 1½- to 2-inch meatballs. This should make 20 to 22 meatballs.
2. Insert the Grill Grate and close the hood. Select GRILL, set the temperature to MED, and set the time to 20 minutes. Select START/STOP to begin preheating.
3. When the unit beeps to signify it has preheated, place the meatballs on the Grill Grate. Close the hood and cook for 10 minutes.
4. After 10 minutes, open the hood and flip the meatballs. Close the hood and cook for 10 minutes more.
5. When cooking is complete, remove the meatballs from the grill. Place the cranberry sauce in a small bowl and use a whisk to stir it into more of a thick jelly sauce. Serve the meatballs with the sauce on the side.

Crispy Dill Pickle Chicken Wings

Servings: 4
Cooking Time: 26 Minutes
Ingredients:

- 2 pounds bone-in chicken wings (drumettes and flats)
- 1½ cups dill pickle juice
- 1½ tablespoons vegetable oil
- ½ tablespoon dried dill
- ¾ teaspoon garlic powder
- Sea salt, to taste
- Freshly ground black pepper, to taste

Directions:

1. Place the chicken wings in a large shallow bowl. Pour the pickle juice over the top, ensuring all of the wings are coated and as submerged as possible. Cover and refrigerate for 2 hours.
2. Insert the Crisper Basket and close the hood. Select AIR CRISP, set the temperature to 390°F, and set the time to 26 minutes. Select START/STOP to begin preheating.
3. While the unit is preheating, rinse the brined chicken wings under cool water, then pat them dry with a paper towel. Place in a large bowl.
4. In a small bowl, whisk together the oil, dill, garlic powder, salt, and pepper. Drizzle over the wings and toss to fully coat them.
5. When the unit beeps to signify it has preheated, place the wings in the basket, spreading them out evenly. Close the hood and AIR CRISP for 11 minutes.
6. After 11 minutes, flip the wings with tongs. Close the hood and AIR CRISP for 11 minutes more.
7. Check the wings for doneness. Cooking is complete when the internal temperature of the chicken reaches at least 165°F on a food thermometer. If needed, AIR CRISP for up to 4 more minutes.
8. Remove the wings from the basket and serve immediately.

Salsa Verde Chicken Enchiladas

Servings: 4
Cooking Time: 20 Minutes
Ingredients:

- 1 tablespoon chili powder
- 1 teaspoon onion powder
- 1 teaspoon garlic powder
- 1 teaspoon ground cumin
- 2 teaspoons salt
- 3 boneless, skinless chicken breasts (about 1½ pounds)
- Extra-virgin olive oil
- 1 (16-ounce) jar salsa verde
- 2 cups shredded Mexican-style cheese blend
- 6 (8-inch) flour tortillas
- Diced tomatoes, for topping
- Sour cream, for topping

Directions:

1. Insert the Grill Grate and close the hood. Select GRILL, set the temperature to MED, and set the time to 12 minutes. Select START/STOP to begin preheating.
2. While the unit is preheating, in a small bowl, combine the chili powder, onion powder, garlic powder, ground cumin, and salt. Drizzle the chicken breasts with the olive oil and season the meat on both sides with the seasoning mixture.
3. When the unit beeps to signify it has preheated, place the chicken breasts on the Grill Grate. Close the hood and cook for 6 minutes.
4. After 6 minutes, open the hood and flip the chicken. Close the hood and cook for 6 minutes more.
5. When cooking is complete, open the hood and use grill mitts to remove the Grill Grate and chicken breasts. Let the chicken breasts cool for about 5 minutes. Use two forks to shred the chicken, or cut it into small chunks.
6. To assemble the enchiladas, place a generous amount of chicken on a tortilla. Lift one end of the tortilla and roll it over and around the chicken. Do not fold in the sides of the tortilla as you roll. Place the enchilada, seam-side down, in the Cooking Pot. Repeat with the remaining 5 tortillas and the rest of the chicken. Pour the salsa verde over the enchiladas, completely covering them. Top the salsa with the shredded cheese.
7. Select BAKE, set the temperature to 350°F, and set the time to 8 minutes. Select START/STOP and then press the PREHEAT button to skip preheating. Close the hood and cook for 8 minutes.
8. When cooking is complete, remove the enchiladas from the pot and serve topped with the diced tomatoes and sour cream.

Turkey Jerky

Servings: 2
Cooking Time: 3 To 5 Hours
Ingredients:
- 1 pound turkey breast, very thinly sliced
- 1 cup soy sauce
- 2 tablespoons light brown sugar, packed
- 2 tablespoons Worcestershire sauce
- ½ teaspoon garlic powder
- ½ teaspoon onion powder
- ½ teaspoon red pepper flakes

Directions:
1. In a resealable bag, combine the turkey, soy sauce, brown sugar, Worcestershire sauce, garlic powder, onion powder, and red pepper flakes. Massage the turkey slices so all are fully coated in the marinade. Seal the bag and refrigerate overnight.
2. An hour before you plan to put the turkey in the dehydrator, remove the turkey slices from the marinade and place them between two paper towels to dry out and come to room temperature.
3. Once dried, lay the turkey slices flat in the Crisper Basket in a single layer. Insert the Crisper Basket in the Cooking Pot and close the hood. Select DEHYDRATE, set the temperature to 150°F, and set the time to 5 hours. Select START/STOP.
4. After 3 hours, check for desired doneness. Continue dehydrating for up to 2 more hours, if desired.
5. When cooking is complete, the jerky should have a dry texture. Remove from the basket and serve, or store in a resealable bag in the refrigerator for up to 2 weeks.

Stuffed Spinach Chicken Breast

Servings: 6
Cooking Time: 12 Minutes
Ingredients:
- 6 ounces cream cheese, at room temperature
- 1 teaspoon salt
- ½ teaspoon freshly ground black pepper
- ¼ cup mayonnaise
- 2 teaspoons garlic powder
- ½ cup grated Parmesan cheese
- 3 cups loosely packed spinach
- 1 teaspoon red pepper flakes (optional)
- 6 (6- to 8-ounce) boneless, skinless chicken breasts, butterflied (see here)
- Avocado oil

Directions:
1. Insert the Grill Grate and close the hood. Select GRILL, set the temperature to HI, and set the time to 12 minutes. Select START/STOP to begin preheating.
2. While the unit is preheating, in a large bowl, combine the cream cheese, salt, pepper, mayonnaise, garlic powder, Parmesan cheese, spinach, and red pepper flakes (if using). Spread the mixture inside the chicken breasts evenly. Close the breasts (like a book), enclosing the stuffing. Drizzle both sides of the chicken breasts with avocado oil for a nice coating.
3. When the unit beeps to signify it has preheated, place the chicken breasts on the Grill Grate. Close the hood and grill for 6 minutes.
4. After 6 minutes, open the hood and flip the chicken. Close the hood and cook for 6 minutes more.
5. When cooking is complete, open the hood and remove the chicken breasts from the grill. Serve.

China Spicy Turkey Thighs

Servings: 6
Cooking Time: 25 Minutes

Ingredients:

- 2 pounds turkey thighs
- 1 teaspoon Chinese five-spice powder
- ¼ teaspoon Sichuan pepper
- 1 teaspoon pink Himalayan salt
- 1 tablespoon Chinese rice vinegar
- 1 tablespoon mustard
- 1 tablespoon chili sauce
- 2 tablespoons soy sauce
- Cooking spray

Directions:

1. Spritz the Crisper Basket with cooking spray.
2. Insert the Crisper Basket and close the hood. Select AIR CRISP, set the temperature to 360ºF, and set the time to 22 minutes. Select START/STOP to begin preheating.
3. Rub the turkey thighs with five-spice powder, Sichuan pepper, and salt on a clean work surface.
4. Put the turkey thighs in the basket and spritz with cooking spray. You may need to work in batches to avoid overcrowding.
5. Close the hood and AIR CRISP for 22 minutes or until well browned. Flip the thighs at least three times during the cooking.
6. Meanwhile, heat the remaining ingredients in a saucepan over medium-high heat. Cook for 3 minutes or until the sauce is thickened and reduces to two thirds.
7. Transfer the thighs onto a plate and baste with sauce before serving.

Meats

Cheesy Beef Meatballs

Servings: 6
Cooking Time: 18 Minutes
Ingredients:
- 1 pound ground beef
- ½ cup grated Parmesan cheese
- 1 tablespoon minced garlic
- ½ cup Mozzarella cheese
- 1 teaspoon freshly ground pepper

Directions:
1. Insert the Crisper Basket and close the hood. Select AIR CRISP, set the temperature to 400°F, and set the time to 18 minutes. Select START/STOP to begin preheating.
2. In a bowl, mix all the ingredients together.
3. Roll the meat mixture into 5 generous meatballs. Transfer to the basket.
4. Close the hood and AIR CRISP for 18 minutes.
5. Serve immediately.

Easy Beef Schnitzel

Servings: 1
Cooking Time: 12 Minutes
Ingredients:
- ½ cup friendly bread crumbs
- 2 tablespoons olive oil
- Pepper and salt, to taste
- 1 egg, beaten
- 1 thin beef schnitzel

Directions:
1. Insert the Crisper Basket and close the hood. Select AIR CRISP, set the temperature to 350°F, and set the time to 12 minutes. Select START/STOP to begin preheating.
2. In a shallow dish, combine the bread crumbs, oil, pepper, and salt.
3. In a second shallow dish, place the beaten egg.
4. Dredge the schnitzel in the egg before rolling it in the bread crumbs.
5. Put the coated schnitzel in the Crisper Basket. Close the hood and AIR CRISP for 12 minutes. Flip the schnitzel halfway through.
6. Serve immediately.

Grilled Pork Banh Mi

Servings: 6
Cooking Time: 15 Minutes
Ingredients:
- 3 tablespoons light brown sugar, packed
- 1 tablespoon soy sauce
- 3 tablespoons minced garlic
- Juice of 2 limes
- 1 shallot, finely minced
- 2 pounds pork tenderloin, cut into 1-inch-thick slices
- 1 daikon radish, cut into thin strips
- 1 large carrot, cut into thin strips
- 3 tablespoons rice vinegar
- ½ teaspoon kosher salt
- 1 teaspoon granulated sugar
- 6 sandwich-size baguettes
- Mayonnaise
- 1 cucumber, thinly sliced
- Fresh cilantro
- 1 jalapeño, sliced

Directions:
1. In a large bowl, combine the brown sugar, soy sauce, garlic, lime juice, shallot, and pork tenderloin slices. Marinate for at least 30 minutes. If marinating for longer, cover and refrigerate.
2. Insert the Cooking Pot and close the hood. Select GRILL, set the temperature to HI, and set the time to 15 minutes. Select START/STOP to begin preheating.
3. While the unit is preheating, in a medium bowl, combine the daikon, carrot, rice vinegar, salt, and sugar.
4. When the unit beeps to signify it has preheated, place the pork in the Cooking Pot. Feel free to add a little bit of the marinade to the pot. Close the hood and cook for 8 minutes.
5. After 8 minutes, open the hood and stir the pork. Close the hood and cook for 7 minutes more.
6. When cooking is complete, slice open each baguette and spread mayonnaise on both sides. Add a layer each of pork, pickled daikon and carrot, cucumber, cilantro, and jalapeño slices and serve.

Baby Back Ribs In Gochujang Marinade

Servings: 4
Cooking Time: 22 Minutes
Ingredients:
- ¼ cup gochujang paste
- ¼ cup soy sauce
- ¼ cup freshly squeezed orange juice
- 2 tablespoons apple cider vinegar
- 2 tablespoons sesame oil
- 6 garlic cloves, minced
- 1½ tablespoons brown sugar
- 1 tablespoon grated fresh ginger
- 1 teaspoon salt
- 4 baby back ribs

Directions:
1. In a medium bowl, add the gochujang paste, soy sauce, orange juice, vinegar, oil, garlic, sugar, ginger, and salt, and stir to combine.
2. Place the baby back ribs on a baking sheet and coat all sides with the sauce. Cover with aluminum foil and refrigerate for 6 hours.
3. Insert the Grill Grate and close the hood. Select GRILL, set the temperature to MEDIUM, and set the time to 22 minutes. Select START/STOP to begin preheating.
4. When the unit beeps to signify it has preheated, place the ribs on the Grill Grate. Close the hood and GRILL for 11 minutes. After 11 minutes, flip the ribs, close the hood, and GRILL for an additional 11 minutes.
5. When cooking is complete, serve immediately.

Honey-caramelized Pork Tenderloin

Servings: 4
Cooking Time: 15 To 20 Minutes
Ingredients:

- 2 tablespoons honey
- 1 tablespoon soy sauce
- ½ teaspoon garlic powder
- ½ teaspoon sea salt
- 1 pork tenderloin

Directions:

1. Insert the Grill Grate and close the hood. Select GRILL, set the temperature to MEDIUM, and set the time to 20 minutes. Select START/STOP to begin preheating.
2. Meanwhile, in a small bowl, combine the honey, soy sauce, garlic powder, and salt.
3. When the unit beeps to signify it has preheated, place the pork tenderloin on the Grill Grate. Baste all sides with the honey glaze. Close the hood and GRILL for 8 minutes. After 8 minutes, flip the pork tenderloin and baste with any remaining glaze. Close the hood and GRILL for 7 minutes more.
4. Cooking is complete when the internal temperature of the pork reaches 145ºF on a food thermometer. If needed, GRILL for up to 5 minutes more.
5. Remove the pork, and set it on a cutting board to rest for 5 minutes. Slice and serve.

Uncle's Famous Tri-tip

Servings: 6 To 8
Cooking Time: 20 Minutes
Ingredients:

- ¼ cup avocado oil
- ½ cup red wine vinegar
- ¼ cup light brown sugar, packed
- 4 tablespoons honey mustard
- 1 tablespoon garlic powder
- 1 tablespoon onion powder
- 1 tablespoon paprika
- 1 tablespoon salt
- 1 tablespoon freshly ground black pepper
- 3 pounds tri-tip

Directions:

1. In a large resealable bag, combine the avocado oil, red wine vinegar, brown sugar, honey mustard, garlic powder, onion powder, paprika, salt, and pepper. Add the tri-tip, seal, and massage the mixture into the meat. Refrigerate overnight.
2. About 20 minutes before grilling, remove the bag from the refrigerator so the marinade becomes liquid again at room temperature.
3. Plug the thermometer into the unit. Insert the Grill Grate and close the hood. Select GRILL, set the temperature to MED, and select PRESET. Use the arrows to the right to select BEEF, then choose desired doneness. Insert the Smart Thermometer into the thickest part of the meat. Select START/STOP to begin preheating.
4. When the unit beeps to signify it has preheated, place the tri-tip on the Grill Grate, fat-side up. Close the hood to begin cooking.
5. When the Foodi™ Grill indicates it is time to flip, open the hood and flip the tri-tip. Close the hood and continue cooking until the Smart Thermometer indicates your desired internal temperature has been reached.
6. When cooking is complete, remove the tri-tip from the grill. Let rest for 10 minutes before slicing against the grain. Serve.

Balsamic Honey Mustard Lamb Chops

Servings: 4 To 6
Cooking Time: 45 Minutes To 1 Hour
Ingredients:

- ¼ cup avocado oil
- ½ cup balsamic vinegar
- 2 garlic cloves, minced
- 1 teaspoon salt
- ½ teaspoon freshly ground black pepper
- 2 tablespoons honey
- 1 tablespoon yellow mustard
- 1 tablespoon fresh rosemary
- 1 (2- to 3-pound) rack of lamb

Directions:

1. In a large bowl, whisk together the avocado oil, vinegar, garlic, salt, pepper, honey, mustard, and rosemary. Add the lamb and massage and coat all sides of the meat with the marinade. Cover and refrigerate for at least 1 hour.
2. Plug the thermometer into the unit. Insert the Cooking Pot and close the hood. Select ROAST, set the temperature to 350°F, and select PRESET. Use the arrows to the right to select BEEF/ LAMB. The unit will default to WELL to cook lamb to a safe temperature. Insert the Smart Thermometer in the thickest part of the lamb without touching bone. Select START/STOP to begin preheating.
3. When the unit beeps to signify it has preheated, place the rack of lamb in the Cooking Pot. Close the hood to begin cooking.
4. When cooking is complete, the Smart Thermometer will indicate that the specified internal temperature has been reached. Remove the lamb from the pot and serve.

Teriyaki Pork And Mushroom Rolls

Servings: 6
Cooking Time: 8 Minutes
Ingredients:

- 4 tablespoons brown sugar
- 4 tablespoons mirin
- 4 tablespoons soy sauce
- 1 teaspoon almond flour
- 2-inch ginger, chopped
- 6 pork belly slices
- 6 ounces Enoki mushrooms

Directions:

1. Mix the brown sugar, mirin, soy sauce, almond flour, and ginger together until brown sugar dissolves.
2. Take pork belly slices and wrap around a bundle of mushrooms. Brush each roll with teriyaki sauce. Chill for half an hour.
3. Insert the Crisper Basket and close the hood. Select AIR CRISP, set the temperature to 350ºF, and set the time to 8 minutes. Select START/STOP to begin preheating.
4. Add marinated pork rolls to the basket.
5. Close the hood and AIR CRISP for 8 minutes. Flip the rolls halfway through.
6. Serve immediately.

Tomato And Lamb Stew

Servings: 6
Cooking Time: 1 Hour
Ingredients:

- 2 tablespoons unsalted butter
- 1 yellow onion, diced
- 4 garlic cloves, minced
- 2 pounds lamb shoulder roast, cut into 1-inch cubes
- 3 cups beef broth
- 1 large potato, cubed
- 1 medium carrot, sliced
- 3 bay leaves
- Salt
- Freshly ground black pepper
- 1 (8-ounce) can tomato sauce
- 1 red bell pepper, chopped
- 1 green bell pepper, chopped

Directions:
1. Insert the Cooking Pot and close the hood. Select ROAST, set the temperature to 350°F, and set the time to 1 hour. Select START/STOP to begin preheating.
2. When the unit beeps to signify it has preheated, place the butter, onion, and garlic in the Cooking Pot. Then add the lamb and stir with a wooden spoon. Close the hood and cook for 10 minutes.
3. After 10 minutes, open the hood and add the beef broth, potato, carrot, and bay leaves, and then season with salt and pepper. Stir to combine. Close the hood and cook for 20 minutes.
4. After 20 minutes, open the hood and stir in the tomato sauce. Close the hood and cook for 10 minutes. After 10 minutes, open the hood and stir. Close the hood and cook for 10 minutes. After 10 minutes, open the hood and add the bell peppers. Close the hood and cook for 10 minutes more.
5. When cooking is complete, open the hood, stir the stew, and remove the bay leaves. Transfer to bowls and serve.

Lamb Rack With Pistachio

Servings: 2
Cooking Time: 20 Minutes
Ingredients:

- ½ cup finely chopped pistachios
- 1 teaspoon chopped fresh rosemary
- 3 tablespoons panko breadcrumbs
- 2 teaspoons chopped fresh oregano
- 1 tablespoon olive oil
- Salt and freshly ground black pepper, to taste
- 1 lamb rack, bones fat trimmed and frenched
- 1 tablespoon Dijon mustard

Directions:
1. Insert the Crisper Basket and close the hood. Select AIR CRISP, set the temperature to 380°F, and set the time to 12 minutes. Select START/STOP to begin preheating.
2. Put the pistachios, rosemary, breadcrumbs, oregano, olive oil, salt, and black pepper in a food processor. Pulse to combine until smooth.
3. Rub the lamb rack with salt and black pepper on a clean work surface, then place it in the basket.
4. Close the hood and AIR CRISP for 12 minutes or until lightly browned. Flip the lamb halfway through the cooking time.
5. Transfer the lamb to a plate and brush with Dijon mustard on the fat side, then sprinkle with the pistachios mixture over the lamb rack to coat well.
6. Put the lamb rack back to the basket. Close the hood and AIR CRISP for 8 more minutes or until the internal temperature of the rack reaches at least 145°F.
7. Remove the lamb rack from the grill with tongs and allow to cool for 5 minutes before sling to serve.

Simple Pork Meatballs With Red Chili

Servings: 4
Cooking Time: 15 Minutes
Ingredients:

- 1 pound ground pork
- 2 cloves garlic, finely minced
- 1 cup scallions, finely chopped
- 1½ tablespoons Worcestershire sauce
- ½ teaspoon freshly grated ginger root
- 1 teaspoon turmeric powder
- 1 tablespoon oyster sauce
- 1 small sliced red chili, for garnish
- Cooking spray

Directions:

1. Spritz the Crisper Basket with cooking spray.
2. Insert the Crisper Basket and close the hood. Select AIR CRISP, set the temperature to 350°F, and set the time to 15 minutes. Select START/STOP to begin preheating.
3. Combine all the ingredients, except for the red chili in a large bowl. Toss to mix well.
4. Shape the mixture into equally sized balls, then arrange them in the basket and spritz with cooking spray.
5. Close the hood and AIR CRISP for 15 minutes or until the balls are lightly browned. Flip the balls halfway through.
6. Serve the pork meatballs with red chili on top.

Spiced Flank Steak

Servings: 2
Cooking Time: 8 Minutes
Ingredients:

- 1 tablespoon chili powder
- 1 teaspoon dried oregano
- 2 teaspoons ground cumin
- 1 teaspoon sea salt
- ¼ teaspoon freshly ground black pepper
- 2 flank steaks

Directions:

1. Insert the Grill Grate and close the hood. Select GRILL, set the temperature to HIGH, and set the time to 8 minutes. Select START/STOP to begin preheating.
2. In a small bowl, mix together the chili powder, oregano, cumin, salt, and pepper. Use your hands to rub the spice mixture on all sides of the steaks.
3. When the unit beeps to signify it has preheated, place the steaks on the Grill Grate. Gently press the steaks down to maximize grill marks. Close the hood and GRILL for 4 minutes. After 4 minutes, flip the steaks, close the hood, and GRILL for 4 minutes more.
4. Remove the steaks from the grill, and transfer them to a cutting board. Let rest for 5 minutes before slicing and serving.

Char Siew

Servings: 4 To 6
Cooking Time: 20 Minutes
Ingredients:

- 1 strip of pork shoulder butt with a good amount of fat marbling
- Olive oil, for brushing the pan
- Marinade:
- 1 teaspoon sesame oil
- 4 tablespoons raw honey
- 1 teaspoon low-sodium dark soy sauce
- 1 teaspoon light soy sauce
- 1 tablespoon rose wine
- 2 tablespoons Hoisin sauce

Directions:

1. Combine all the marinade ingredients together in a Ziploc bag. Put pork in bag, making sure all sections of pork strip are engulfed in the marinade. Chill for 3 to 24 hours.
2. Take out the strip 30 minutes before planning to roast.
3. Select ROAST, set the temperature to 350°F, and set the time to 20 minutes. Select START/STOP to begin preheating.
4. Put foil on the pot and brush with olive oil. Put marinated pork strip onto prepared pot.
5. Close the hood and ROAST for 20 minutes.
6. Glaze with marinade every 5 to 10 minutes.
7. Remove strip and leave to cool a few minutes before slicing.
8. Serve immediately.

Pork Spareribs With Peanut Sauce

Servings: 6
Cooking Time: 30 Minutes
Ingredients:

- 2 (2- to 3-pound) racks St. Louis–style spareribs
- Sea salt
- ½ cup crunchy peanut butter
- 1 tablespoon rice vinegar
- 2 tablespoons hoisin sauce
- 1 tablespoon honey
- 2 tablespoons soy sauce
- 1 teaspoon garlic powder

Directions:
1.   Plug the thermometer into the unit. Insert the Grill Grate and close the hood. Select GRILL, set the temperature to MED, and select PRESET. Use the arrows to the right to select PORK. The unit will default to WELL to cook the pork to a safe temperature. Insert the Smart Thermometer into the thickest part of the meat between two bones, making sure it does not touch bone. Select START/STOP to begin preheating.
2.   When the unit beeps to signify it has preheated, place the racks of ribs on the Grill Grate. Close the hood to begin cooking.
3.   When the Foodi™ Grill indicates it's time to flip, open the hood and flip the racks. Then close the hood to continue cooking.
4.   While the ribs are cooking, in a small bowl, combine the peanut butter, vinegar, hoisin sauce, honey, soy sauce, and garlic powder and mix until well blended.
5.   When cooking is complete, the Smart Thermometer will indicate that the desired internal temperature has been reached. Open the hood and remove the ribs. Either pour the sauce over the ribs or divide the sauce between individual bowls for dipping. Serve.

Miso Marinated Steak

Servings: 4
Cooking Time: 12 Minutes
Ingredients:

- ¾ pound flank steak
- 1½ tablespoons sake
- 1 tablespoon brown miso paste
- 1 teaspoon honey
- 2 cloves garlic, pressed
- 1 tablespoon olive oil

Directions:
1.   Put all the ingredients in a Ziploc bag. Shake to cover the steak well with the seasonings and refrigerate for at least 1 hour.
2.   Insert the Crisper Basket and close the hood. Select AIR CRISP, set the temperature to 400°F, and set the time to 12 minutes. Select START/STOP to begin preheating.
3.   Coat all sides of the steak with cooking spray. Put the steak in the basket.
4.   Close the hood and AIR CRISP for 12 minutes, turning the steak twice during the cooking time, then serve immediately.

Ranch And Cheddar Pork Chops

Servings: 6
Cooking Time: 10 Minutes
Ingredients:

- 8 ounces cream cheese, at room temperature
- 1 tablespoon ranch seasoning mix
- ½ cup shredded cheddar cheese
- 6 (6-ounce) boneless pork chops

Directions:
1.   Insert the Grill Grate and close the hood. Select GRILL, set the temperature to HI, and set the time to 10 minutes. Select START/STOP to begin preheating.
2.   While the unit is preheating, in a small bowl, combine the cream cheese, ranch seasoning, and cheddar cheese.
3.   When the unit beeps to signify it has preheated, place the pork chops on the Grill Grate. Close the hood and grill for 5 minutes.
4.   After 5 minutes, open the hood and flip the chops. Then top each with the ranch-cheese mixture. Close the hood and cook for 5 minutes more.
5.   When cooking is complete, remove the chops from the grill and serve.

Crispy Pork Tenderloin

Servings: 6
Cooking Time: 10 Minutes
Ingredients:
- 2 large egg whites
- 1½ tablespoons Dijon mustard
- 2 cups crushed pretzel crumbs
- 1½ pounds pork tenderloin, cut into ¼-pound sections
- Cooking spray

Directions:
1. Spritz the Crisper Basket with cooking spray.
2. Insert the Crisper Basket and close the hood. Select AIR CRISP, set the temperature to 350ºF, and set the time to 10 minutes. Select START/STOP to begin preheating.
3. Whisk the egg whites with Dijon mustard in a bowl until bubbly. Pour the pretzel crumbs in a separate bowl.
4. Dredge the pork tenderloin in the egg white mixture and press to coat. Shake the excess off and roll the tenderloin over the pretzel crumbs.
5. Arrange the well-coated pork tenderloin in batches in a single layer in the Crisper Basket and spritz with cooking spray.
6. Close the hood and AIR CRISP for 10 minutes or until the pork is golden brown and crispy. Flip the pork halfway through. Repeat with remaining pork sections.
7. Serve immediately.

Pork Chops In Bourbon

Servings: 4
Cooking Time: 35 Minutes
Ingredients:
- 2 cups ketchup
- ¾ cup bourbon
- ¼ cup apple cider vinegar
- ¼ cup soy sauce
- 1 cup packed brown sugar
- 3 tablespoons Worcestershire sauce
- ½ tablespoon dry mustard powder
- 4 boneless pork chops
- Sea salt, to taste
- Freshly ground black pepper, to taste

Directions:
1. In a medium saucepan over high heat, combine the ketchup, bourbon, vinegar, soy sauce, sugar, Worcestershire sauce, and mustard powder. Stir to combine and bring to a boil.
2. Reduce the heat to low and simmer, uncovered and stirring occasionally, for 20 minutes. The barbecue sauce will thicken while cooking. Once thickened, remove the pan from the heat and set aside.
3. While the barbecue sauce is cooking, insert the Grill Grate into the unit and close the hood. Select GRILL, set the temperature to MEDIUM, and set the time to 15 minutes. Select START/STOP to begin preheating.
4. When the unit beeps to signify it has preheated, place the pork chops on the Grill Grate. Close the hood, and GRILL for 8 minutes. After 8 minutes, flip the pork chops and baste the cooked side with the barbecue sauce. Close the hood, and GRILL for 5 minutes more.
5. Open the hood, and flip the pork chops again, basting both sides with the barbecue sauce. Close the hood, and GRILL for the final 2 minutes.
6. When cooking is complete, season with salt and pepper and serve immediately.

Potato And Prosciutto Salad

Servings: 8
Cooking Time: 7 Minutes
Ingredients:
- Salad:
- 4 pounds potatoes, boiled and cubed
- 15 slices prosciutto, diced
- 2 cups shredded Cheddar cheese
- Dressing:
- 15 ounces sour cream
- 2 tablespoons mayonnaise
- 1 teaspoon salt
- 1 teaspoon black pepper
- 1 teaspoon dried basil

Directions:
1. Select AIR CRISP, set the temperature to 350°F, and set the time to 7 minutes. Select START/STOP to begin preheating.
2. Put the potatoes, prosciutto, and Cheddar in a baking pan. Place the pan directly in the pot. Close the hood and AIR CRISP for 7 minutes.
3. In a separate bowl, mix the sour cream, mayonnaise, salt, pepper, and basil using a whisk.
4. Coat the salad with the dressing and serve.

Vietnamese Pork Chops

Servings: 2
Cooking Time: 12 Minutes
Ingredients:
- 1 tablespoon chopped shallot
- 1 tablespoon chopped garlic
- 1 tablespoon fish sauce
- 3 tablespoons lemongrass
- 1 teaspoon soy sauce
- 1 tablespoon brown sugar
- 1 tablespoon olive oil
- 1 teaspoon ground black pepper
- 2 pork chops

Directions:
1. Combine shallot, garlic, fish sauce, lemongrass, soy sauce, brown sugar, olive oil, and pepper in a bowl. Stir to mix well.
2. Put the pork chops in the bowl. Toss to coat well. Place the bowl in the refrigerator to marinate for 2 hours.
3. Insert the Crisper Basket and close the hood. Select AIR CRISP, set the temperature to 400°F, and set the time to 12 minutes. Select START/STOP to begin preheating.
4. Remove the pork chops from the bowl and discard the marinade. Transfer the chops into the basket.
5. Close the hood and AIR CRISP for 12 minutes or until lightly browned. Flip the pork chops halfway through the cooking time.
6. Remove the pork chops from the basket and serve hot.

Citrus Carnitas

Servings: 6
Cooking Time: 25 Minutes
Ingredients:
- 2½ pounds boneless country-style pork ribs, cut into 2-inch pieces
- 3 tablespoons olive brine
- 1 tablespoon minced fresh oregano leaves
- ⅓ cup orange juice
- 1 teaspoon ground cumin
- 1 tablespoon minced garlic
- 1 teaspoon salt
- 1 teaspoon ground black pepper
- Cooking spray

Directions:
1. Combine all the ingredients in a large bowl. Toss to coat the pork ribs well. Wrap the bowl in plastic and refrigerate for at least an hour to marinate.
2. Spritz the Crisper Basket with cooking spray.
3. Insert the Crisper Basket and close the hood. Select AIR CRISP, set the temperature to 400ºF, and set the time to 25 minutes. Select START/STOP to begin preheating.
4. Arrange the marinated pork ribs in a single layer in the basket and spritz with cooking spray.
5. Close the hood and AIR CRISP for 25 minutes or until well browned. Flip the ribs halfway through.
6. Serve immediately.

Golden Wasabi Spam

Servings: 3
Cooking Time: 12 Minutes
Ingredients:
- ⅔ cup all-purpose flour
- 2 large eggs
- 1½ tablespoons wasabi paste
- 2 cups panko breadcrumbs
- 6 ½-inch-thick spam slices
- Cooking spray

Directions:
1. Spritz the Crisper Basket with cooking spray.
2. Insert the Crisper Basket and close the hood. Select AIR CRISP, set the temperature to 400ºF, and set the time to 12 minutes. Select START/STOP to begin preheating.
3. Pour the flour in a shallow plate. Whisk the eggs with wasabi in a large bowl. Pour the panko in a separate shallow plate.
4. Dredge the spam slices in the flour first, then dunk in the egg mixture, and then roll the spam over the panko to coat well. Shake the excess off.
5. Arrange the spam slices in a single layer in the basket and spritz with cooking spray.
6. Close the hood and AIR CRISP for 12 minutes or until the spam slices are golden and crispy. Flip the spam slices halfway through.
7. Serve immediately.

Cheesy Jalapeño Popper Burgers

Servings: 4
Cooking Time: 9 Minutes
Ingredients:

- 2 jalapeño peppers, seeded, stemmed, and minced
- ½ cup shredded Cheddar cheese
- 4 ounces cream cheese, at room temperature
- 4 slices bacon, cooked and crumbled
- 2 pounds ground beef
- ½ teaspoon chili powder
- ¼ teaspoon paprika
- ¼ teaspoon freshly ground black pepper
- 4 hamburger buns
- 4 slices pepper Jack cheese
- Lettuce, sliced tomato, and sliced red onion, for topping (optional)

Directions:

1. Insert the Grill Grate and close the hood. Select GRILL, set the temperature to HIGH, and set the time to 9 minutes. Select START/STOP to begin preheating.
2. In a medium bowl, combine the peppers, Cheddar cheese, cream cheese, and bacon until well combined.
3. Form the ground beef into 8¼-inch-thick patties. Spoon some of the filling mixture onto four of the patties, then place a second patty on top of each to make four burgers. Use your fingers to pinch the edges of the patties together to seal in the filling. Reshape the patties with your hands as needed.
4. Combine the chili powder, paprika, and pepper in a small bowl. Sprinkle the mixture onto both sides of the burgers.
5. When the units beeps to signify it has preheated, place the burgers on the Grill Grate. Close the hood and GRILL for 4 minutes without flipping. Cooking is complete when the internal temperature of the beef reaches at least 145ºF on a food thermometer. If needed, GRILL for up to 5 more minutes.
6. Place the burgers on the hamburger buns and top with pepper Jack cheese. Add lettuce, tomato, and red onion, if desired.

Stuffed-onion Burgers

Servings: 6
Cooking Time: 15 Minutes
Ingredients:

- 2 large red onions
- 1 teaspoon onion powder
- 1 teaspoon garlic powder
- 2 teaspoons sea salt
- 2 teaspoons freshly ground black pepper
- 4 tablespoons gluten-free Worcestershire sauce
- 2 pounds ground beef

Directions:

1. Cut both ends off the onions. Slice each onion crosswise into thirds and peel off the papery outer skin. Separate the outer two rings (keeping the pair together) from each third for a stable and firm onion ring wrapper.
2. Insert the Grill Grate and close the hood. Select GRILL, set the temperature to HI, and set the time to 15 minutes. Select START/STOP to begin preheating.
3. In a large bowl, combine the onion powder, garlic powder, salt, pepper, and Worcestershire sauce. Add the ground beef in chunks and loosely mix. Form the mixture into 6 equal-size patties. Stuff the burger patties into the onion rings and make a small indentation in the middle of each patty with your thumb.
4. When the unit beeps to signify it has preheated, place the patties on the Grill Grate. Close the hood and grill for 7 minutes, 30 seconds.
5. After 7 minutes, 30 seconds, open the hood and flip the burgers. Close the hood and cook for 7 minutes, 30 seconds more for medium-well burgers. If you prefer your burgers more well-done, continue cooking to your liking.
6. When cooking is complete, remove the burgers from the grill and serve.

Korean Bbq Beef

Servings: 4
Cooking Time: 5 Minutes
Ingredients:

- ⅓ cup soy sauce
- 2 tablespoons sesame oil
- 2½ tablespoons brown sugar
- 3 garlic cloves, minced
- ½ teaspoon freshly ground black pepper
- 1 pound rib eye steak, thinly sliced
- 2 scallions, thinly sliced, for garnish
- Toasted sesame seeds, for garnish

Directions:

1. In a small bowl, whisk together the soy sauce, sesame oil, brown sugar, garlic, and black pepper until fully combined.
2. Place the beef into a large shallow bowl, and pour the sauce over the slices. Cover and refrigerate for 1 hour.
3. Insert the Grill Grate and close the hood. Select GRILL, set the temperature to MEDIUM, and set the time to 5 minutes. Select START/STOP to begin preheating.
4. When the unit beeps to signify it has preheated, place the beef onto the Grill Grate. Close the hood and GRILL for 4 minutes without flipping.
5. After 4 minutes, check the steak for desired doneness, grilling for up to 1 minute more, if desired.
6. When cooking is complete, top with scallions and sesame seeds and serve immediately.

Citrus Pork Loin Roast

Servings: 8
Cooking Time: 45 Minutes
Ingredients:

- 1 tablespoon lime juice
- 1 tablespoon orange marmalade
- 1 teaspoon coarse brown mustard
- 1 teaspoon curry powder
- 1 teaspoon dried lemongrass
- 2 pound boneless pork loin roast
- Salt and ground black pepper, to taste
- Cooking spray

Directions:

1. Insert the Crisper Basket and close the hood. Select AIR CRISP, set the temperature to 360ºF, and set the time to 45 minutes. Select START/STOP to begin preheating.
2. Mix the lime juice, marmalade, mustard, curry powder, and lemongrass.
3. Rub mixture all over the surface of the pork loin. Season with salt and pepper.
4. Spray the Crisper Basket with cooking spray and place pork roast diagonally in the basket.
5. Close the hood and AIR CRISP for 45 minutes, until the internal temperature reaches at least 145ºF.
6. Wrap roast in foil and let rest for 10 minutes before slicing.
7. Serve immediately.

Hamburger Steak With Mushroom Gravy

Servings: 4
Cooking Time: 18 Minutes
Ingredients:

- For the hamburger steaks
- 1 cup plain bread crumbs
- 2 tablespoons Worcestershire sauce
- 1 teaspoon onion powder
- 1 teaspoon garlic powder
- 1 large egg
- 1 teaspoon granulated sugar
- 1 teaspoon salt
- ¼ teaspoon freshly ground black pepper
- 1 pound ground beef
- For the mushroom gravy
- 2 cups beef broth
- 4 tablespoons (½ stick) unsalted butter
- 8 ounces white mushrooms, sliced
- 1 tablespoon Worcestershire sauce
- 4 tablespoons all-purpose flour
- Salt
- Freshly ground black pepper

Directions:

1. Insert the Grill Grate and close the hood. Select GRILL, set the temperature to HI, and set the time to 10 minutes. Select START/STOP to begin preheating.
2. While the unit is preheating, in a large bowl, combine the bread crumbs, Worcestershire sauce, onion powder, garlic powder, egg, sugar, salt, and pepper. Add the ground beef in chunks and loosely mix until just combined. Form the mixture into 4 equal-sized patties.
3. When the unit beeps to signify it has preheated, place the beef patties on the Grill Grate. Close the hood and grill for 5 minutes.
4. While the patties are cooking, gather and measure the ingredients for the gravy.
5. After 5 minutes, open the hood and flip the burgers. Close the hood and cook for 5 minutes more.
6. When cooking is complete, use grill mitts to remove the Grill Grate and burgers from the unit.
7. Add the beef broth, butter, mushrooms, and Worcestershire sauce to the Cooking Pot. Select GRILL, set the temperature to HI, and set the time to 8 minutes. Select START/STOP and then press the PREHEAT button to skip preheating. Close the hood and cook for 4 minutes.
8. After 4 minutes, open the hood and stir in the flour. Mix well. Close the hood and cook for 4 minutes more.
9. When cooking is complete, the sauce will be thickened and the butter will be completely melted. Season with salt and pepper. Pour the mushroom gravy over the hamburger steaks and serve.

Swedish Beef Meatballs

Servings: 8
Cooking Time: 12 Minutes
Ingredients:

- 1 pound ground beef
- 1 egg, beaten
- 2 carrots, shredded
- 2 bread slices, crumbled
- 1 small onion, minced
- ½ teaspoons garlic salt
- Pepper and salt, to taste
- 1 cup tomato sauce
- 2 cups pasta sauce

Directions:

1. Insert the Crisper Basket and close the hood. Select AIR CRISP, set the temperature to 400ºF, and set the time to 7 minutes. Select START/STOP to begin preheating.
2. In a bowl, combine the ground beef, egg, carrots, crumbled bread, onion, garlic salt, pepper and salt.
3. Divide the mixture into equal amounts and shape each one into a small meatball.
4. Put them in the Crisper Basket. Close the hood and AIR CRISP for 7 minutes.
5. Transfer the meatballs to an oven-safe dish and top with the tomato sauce and pasta sauce.
6. Set the dish into the pot and allow to AIR CRISP at 320ºF for 5 more minutes. Serve hot.

Bacon-wrapped Scallops

Servings: 4
Cooking Time: 10 Minutes
Ingredients:

- 8 slices bacon, cut in half
- 16 sea scallops, patted dry
- Cooking spray
- Salt and freshly ground black pepper, to taste
- 16 toothpicks, soaked in water for at least 30 minutes

Directions:

1. Insert the Crisper Basket and close the hood. Select AIR CRISP, set the temperature to 370°F, and set the time to 10 minutes. Select START/STOP to begin preheating.
2. On a clean work surface, wrap half of a slice of bacon around each scallop and secure with a toothpick.
3. Lay the bacon-wrapped scallops in the Crisper Basket in a single layer. You may need to work in batches to avoid overcrowding.
4. Spritz the scallops with cooking spray and sprinkle the salt and pepper to season.
5. Close the hood and AIR CRISP for 10 minutes, flipping the scallops halfway through, or until the bacon is cooked through and the scallops are firm.
6. Remove the scallops from the basket to a plate and repeat with the remaining scallops. Serve warm.

Flank Steak Pinwheels

Servings: 4 To 6
Cooking Time: 10 Minutes
Ingredients:

- 2 pounds flank steak
- Salt
- Freshly ground black pepper
- 4 ounces cream cheese, at room temperature
- 2 tablespoons minced garlic
- ½ cup shredded mozzarella cheese
- 4 tablespoons grated Parmesan cheese
- 2 cups fresh spinach

Directions:

1. Insert the Grill Grate and close the hood. Select GRILL, set the temperature to HI, and set the time to 10 minutes. Select START/STOP to begin preheating.
2. While the unit is preheating, butterfly the steaks and season both sides with salt and pepper. Spread the cream cheese across the cut side of each steak and evenly distribute the garlic over the cream cheese. Layer the mozzarella, Parmesan cheese, and spinach on top. Starting from the bottom of each steak, roll the meat upward tightly over the filling. Use about 6 toothpicks, evenly spaced, to secure the seam. Then slice in between the toothpicks, creating 1½- to 2-inch-thick rolls.
3. When the unit beeps to signify it has preheated, place the pinwheels on the Grill Grate, cut-side down. Close the hood and grill for 5 minutes.
4. After 5 minutes, open the hood and flip the pinwheels. Close the hood and cook for 5 minutes more.
5. When cooking is complete, check the meat for doneness. If you prefer your beef more well done, continue cooking to your liking. Remove the pinwheels from the grill and serve.
6. Cut the steak almost in half from one side (parallel to the cutting board), stopping just before you reach the other side. When you open the steak up, it'll be thinner and have two matching wings like a butterfly.

Meatless

Simple Ratatouille

Servings: 2
Cooking Time: 16 Minutes
Ingredients:
- 2 Roma tomatoes, thinly sliced
- 1 zucchini, thinly sliced
- 2 yellow bell peppers, sliced
- 2 garlic cloves, minced
- 2 tablespoons olive oil
- 2 tablespoons herbes de Provence
- 1 tablespoon vinegar
- Salt and black pepper, to taste

Directions:
1. Select ROAST, set the temperature to 390ºF, and set the time to 16 minutes. Select START/STOP to begin preheating.
2. Place the tomatoes, zucchini, bell peppers, garlic, olive oil, herbes de Provence, and vinegar in a large bowl and toss until the vegetables are evenly coated. Sprinkle with salt and pepper and toss again. Pour the vegetable mixture into the pot.
3. Close the hood and ROAST for 8 minutes. Stir and continue roasting for 8 minutes until tender.
4. Let the vegetable mixture stand for 5 minutes in the basket before removing and serving.

Kidney Beans Oatmeal In Peppers

Servings: 2 To 4
Cooking Time: 6 Minutes
Ingredients:
- 2 large bell peppers, halved lengthwise, deseeded
- 2 tablespoons cooked kidney beans
- 2 tablespoons cooked chick peas
- 2 cups cooked oatmeal
- 1 teaspoon ground cumin
- ½ teaspoon paprika
- ½ teaspoon salt or to taste
- ¼ teaspoon black pepper powder
- ¼ cup yogurt

Directions:
1. Insert the Crisper Basket and close the hood. Select AIR CRISP, set the temperature to 355ºF, and set the time to 6 minutes. Select START/STOP to begin preheating.
2. Put the bell peppers, cut-side down, in the Crisper Basket. Close the hood and AIR CRISP for 2 minutes.
3. Take the peppers out of the grill and let cool.
4. In a bowl, combine the rest of the ingredients.
5. Divide the mixture evenly and use each portion to stuff a pepper.
6. Return the stuffed peppers to the basket. Close the hood and AIR CRISP for 4 minutes.
7. Serve hot.

Hearty Roasted Veggie Salad

Servings: 2
Cooking Time: 20 Minutes
Ingredients:

- 1 potato, chopped
- 1 carrot, sliced diagonally
- 1 cup cherry tomatoes
- ½ small beetroot, sliced
- ¼ onion, sliced
- ½ teaspoon turmeric
- ½ teaspoon cumin
- ¼ teaspoon sea salt
- 2 tablespoons olive oil, divided
- A handful of arugula
- A handful of baby spinach
- Juice of 1 lemon
- 3 tablespoons canned chickpeas, for serving
- Parmesan shavings, for serving

Directions:

1. Insert the Crisper Basket and close the hood. Select ROAST, set the temperature to 370ºF, and set the time to 20 minutes. Select START/STOP to begin preheating.
2. Combine the potato, carrot, cherry tomatoes, beetroot, onion, turmeric, cumin, salt, and 1 tablespoon of olive oil in a large bowl and toss until well coated.
3. Arrange the veggies in the Crisper Basket. Close the hood and ROAST for 20 minutes, shaking the basket halfway through.
4. Let the veggies cool for 5 to 10 minutes in the basket.
5. Put the arugula, baby spinach, lemon juice, and remaining 1 tablespoon of olive oil in a salad bowl and stir to combine. Mix in the roasted veggies and toss well.
6. Scatter the chickpeas and Parmesan shavings on top and serve immediately.

Cashew Stuffed Mushrooms

Servings: 6
Cooking Time: 15 Minutes
Ingredients:

- 1 cup basil
- ½ cup cashew, soaked overnight
- ½ cup nutritional yeast
- 1 tablespoon lemon juice
- 2 cloves garlic
- 1 tablespoon olive oil
- Salt, to taste
- 1 pound baby bella mushroom, stems removed

Directions:

1. Insert the Crisper Basket and close the hood. Select AIR CRISP, set the temperature to 400ºF, and set the time to 15 minutes. Select START/STOP to begin preheating.
2. Prepare the pesto. In a food processor, blend the basil, cashew nuts, nutritional yeast, lemon juice, garlic and olive oil to combine well. Sprinkle with salt, as desired.
3. Turn the mushrooms cap-side down and spread the pesto on the underside of each cap.
4. Transfer to the basket. Close the hood and AIR CRISP for 15 minutes.
5. Serve warm.

Honey-glazed Baby Carrots

Servings: 4
Cooking Time: 12 Minutes
Ingredients:

- 1 pound baby carrots
- 2 tablespoons olive oil
- 1 tablespoon honey
- 1 teaspoon dried dill
- Salt and black pepper, to taste

Directions:

1. Insert the Crisper Basket and close the hood. Select ROAST, set the temperature to 350ºF, and set the time to 12 minutes. Select START/STOP to begin preheating.
2. Place the carrots in a large bowl. Add the olive oil, honey, dill, salt, and pepper and toss to coat well.
3. Arrange the carrots in the Crisper Basket. Close the hood and ROAST for 12 minutes, until crisp-tender. Shake the basket once during cooking.
4. Serve warm.

Chermoula Beet Roast

Servings: 4
Cooking Time: 25 Minutes
Ingredients:

- Chermoula:
- 1 cup packed fresh cilantro leaves
- ½ cup packed fresh parsley leaves
- 6 cloves garlic, peeled
- 2 teaspoons smoked paprika
- 2 teaspoons ground cumin
- 1 teaspoon ground coriander
- ½ to 1 teaspoon cayenne pepper
- Pinch of crushed saffron (optional)
- ½ cup extra-virgin olive oil
- Kosher salt, to taste
- Beets:
- 3 medium beets, trimmed, peeled, and cut into 1-inch chunks
- 2 tablespoons chopped fresh cilantro
- 2 tablespoons chopped fresh parsley

Directions:

1. In a food processor, combine the cilantro, parsley, garlic, paprika, cumin, coriander, and cayenne. Pulse until coarsely chopped. Add the saffron, if using, and process until combined. With the food processor running, slowly add the olive oil in a steady stream; process until the sauce is uniform. Season with salt.
2. Insert the Crisper Basket and close the hood. Select ROAST, set the temperature to 375ºF, and set the time to 25 minutes. Select START/STOP to begin preheating.
3. In a large bowl, drizzle the beets with ½ cup of the chermoula to coat. Arrange the beets in the Crisper Basket. Close the hood and ROAST for 25 minutes, or until the beets are tender.
4. Transfer the beets to a serving platter. Sprinkle with the chopped cilantro and parsley and serve.

Roasted Butternut Squash

Servings: 6 To 8
Cooking Time: 40 Minutes
Ingredients:

- 2 butternut squash
- Avocado oil, for drizzling
- Salt
- Freshly ground black pepper

Directions:

1. Cut off the stem end of each squash, then cut the squash in half lengthwise. To do this, carefully rock the knife back and forth to cut through the tough skin and flesh. Use a spoon to scrape out the seeds from each half.
2. Insert the Cooking Pot and close the hood. Select ROAST, set the temperature to 400°F, and set the time to 40 minutes. Select START/STOP to begin preheating.
3. While the unit is preheating, drizzle the avocado oil over the butternut squash flesh. I also like to rub it in with my hands. Season with salt and pepper.
4. When the unit beeps to signify it has preheated, place the butternut squash in the Cooking Pot, cut-side down. Close the hood and cook for 40 minutes.
5. When cooking is complete, the flesh will be soft and easy to scoop out with a spoon. Remove from the grill and serve.

Cauliflower Steaks With Ranch Dressing

Servings: 2
Cooking Time: 15 Minutes
Ingredients:
- 1 head cauliflower, stemmed and leaves removed
- ¼ cup canola oil
- ½ teaspoon garlic powder
- ½ teaspoon paprika
- Sea salt, to taste
- Freshly ground black pepper, to taste
- 1 cup shredded Cheddar cheese
- Ranch dressing, for garnish
- 4 slices bacon, cooked and crumbled
- 2 tablespoons chopped fresh chives

Directions:
1. Cut the cauliflower from top to bottom into two 2-inch "steaks"; reserve the remaining cauliflower to cook separately.
2. Insert the Grill Grate and close the hood. Select GRILL, set the temperature to MAX, and set the time to 15 minutes. Select START/STOP to begin preheating.
3. Meanwhile, in a small bowl, whisk together the oil, garlic powder, and paprika. Season with salt and pepper. Brush each steak with the oil mixture on both sides.
4. When the unit beeps to signify it has preheated, place the steaks on the Grill Grate. Close the hood and GRILL for 10 minutes.
5. After 10 minutes, flip the steaks and top each with ½ cup of cheese. Close the hood and continue to GRILL until the cheese is melted, about 5 minutes.
6. When cooking is complete, place the cauliflower steaks on a plate and drizzle with the ranch dressing. Top with the bacon and chives.

Parmesan Asparagus Fries

Servings: 4
Cooking Time: 5 To 7 Minutes
Ingredients:
- 2 egg whites
- ¼ cup water
- ¼ cup plus 2 tablespoons grated Parmesan cheese, divided
- ¾ cup panko bread crumbs
- ¼ teaspoon salt
- 12 ounces fresh asparagus spears, woody ends trimmed
- Cooking spray

Directions:
1. Insert the Crisper Basket and close the hood. Select AIR CRISP, set the temperature to 390°F, and set the time to 7 minutes. Select START/STOP to begin preheating.
2. In a shallow dish, whisk together the egg whites and water until slightly foamy. In a separate shallow dish, thoroughly combine ¼ cup of Parmesan cheese, bread crumbs, and salt.
3. Dip the asparagus in the egg white, then roll in the cheese mixture to coat well.
4. Place the asparagus in the Crisper Basket in a single layer, leaving space between each spear. You may need to work in batches to avoid overcrowding.
5. Spritz the asparagus with cooking spray. Close the hood and AIR CRISP for 5 to 7 minutes until golden brown and crisp.
6. Repeat with the remaining asparagus spears.
7. Sprinkle with the remaining 2 tablespoons of cheese and serve hot.

Broccoli And Tofu Teriyaki

Servings: 4
Cooking Time: 8 Minutes
Ingredients:

- 1 (14-ounce) package firm tofu, cut into ½-inch cubes
- 1 medium head broccoli, chopped into florets (3 to 4 cups)
- Extra-virgin olive oil
- 1 cup water
- ⅓ cup soy sauce
- 3 tablespoons light brown sugar, packed
- 1 tablespoon peeled minced fresh ginger
- ¼ teaspoon garlic powder
- 1 teaspoon cornstarch

Directions:

1. Insert the Grill Grate and close the hood. Select GRILL, set the temperature to HI, and set the time to 8 minutes. Select START/STOP to begin preheating.
2. While the unit is preheating, on a large plate, lightly coat the tofu and broccoli florets with extra-virgin olive oil.
3. When the unit beeps to signify it has preheated, place the broccoli and tofu pieces on the Grill Grate. Close the hood and grill for 4 minutes.
4. While the tofu and broccoli are cooking, in a small bowl, mix together the water, soy sauce, brown sugar, ginger, garlic powder, and cornstarch until the sugar and cornstarch are dissolved.
5. After 4 minutes, open the hood and use grill mitts to remove the Grill Grate and the broccoli and tofu. Carefully pour the soy sauce mix into the Cooking Pot and add the broccoli and tofu. Close the hood and cook for 4 minutes more.
6. When cooking is complete, open the hood and stir. Serve.

Honey-glazed Roasted Veggies

Servings:3
Cooking Time: 20 Minutes
Ingredients:

- Glaze:
- 2 tablespoons raw honey
- 2 teaspoons minced garlic
- ¼ teaspoon dried marjoram
- ¼ teaspoon dried basil
- ¼ teaspoon dried oregano
- ⅛ teaspoon dried sage
- ⅛ teaspoon dried rosemary
- ⅛ teaspoon dried thyme
- ½ teaspoon salt
- ¼ teaspoon ground black pepper
- Veggies:
- 3 to 4 medium red potatoes, cut into 1- to 2-inch pieces
- 1 small zucchini, cut into 1- to 2-inch pieces
- 1 small carrot, sliced into ¼-inch rounds
- 1 package cherry tomatoes, halved
- 1 cup sliced mushrooms
- 3 tablespoons olive oil

Directions:

1. Insert the Crisper Basket and close the hood. Select ROAST, set the temperature to 380ºF, and set the time to 15 minutes. Select START/STOP to begin preheating.
2. Combine the honey, garlic, marjoram, basil, oregano, sage, rosemary, thyme, salt, and pepper in a small bowl and stir to mix well. Set aside.
3. Place the red potatoes, zucchini, carrot, cherry tomatoes, and mushroom in a large bowl. Drizzle with the olive oil and toss to coat.
4. Pour the veggies into the Crisper Basket. Close the hood and ROAST for 15 minutes, shaking the basket halfway through.
5. When ready, transfer the roasted veggies to the large bowl. Pour the honey mixture over the veggies, tossing to coat.
6. Spread out the veggies in a baking pan and place in the grill.
7. Increase the temperature to 390ºF and ROAST for an additional 5 minutes, or until the veggies are tender and glazed. Serve warm.

Sweet And Spicy Corn On The Cob

Servings: 6
Cooking Time: 12 Minutes
Ingredients:

- 6 ears corn, shucked
- Avocado oil, for drizzling
- Salt
- Freshly ground black pepper
- ½ cup sweet chili sauce
- ¼ cup sour cream
- ¼ cup mayonnaise
- 2 tablespoons sriracha
- Juice of 1 lime
- ¼ cup chopped cilantro, for garnish

Directions:

1. Insert the Grill Grate and close the hood. Select GRILL, set the temperature to MAX, and set the time to 12 minutes. Select START/STOP to begin preheating.
2. While the unit is preheating, drizzle the corn with avocado oil, rubbing it in to coat. Season with salt and pepper all over.
3. When the unit beeps to signify it has preheated, place the corn on the Grill Grate. Close the hood and grill for 6 minutes.
4. After 6 minutes, open the hood and flip the corn. Close the hood and cook 6 minutes more.
5. While the corn is cooking, in a small bowl, combine the sweet chili sauce, sour cream, mayonnaise, sriracha, and lime juice.
6. When cooking is complete, remove the corn from the grill. Coat the ears with the sweet chili sauce mixture. Garnish with the cilantro and serve.

Crispy Noodle Vegetable Stir-fry

Servings: 4
Cooking Time: 20 Minutes
Ingredients:

- 4 cups water
- 3 (5-ounce) packages instant ramen noodles (flavor packets removed) or 1 (12-ounce) package chow mein noodles
- Extra-virgin olive oil, for drizzling, plus 3 tablespoons
- 3 garlic cloves, minced
- 3 teaspoons peeled minced fresh ginger
- 1 red bell pepper, cut into thin strips
- 4 ounces white mushrooms, sliced
- 1 (8-ounce) can sweet baby corn, drained
- 2 cups snap peas
- 2 cups broccoli florets
- 1 small carrot, diagonally sliced
- 1 cup vegetable broth
- 1 cup soy sauce
- ¼ cup rice vinegar
- 1 tablespoon sesame oil
- 3 tablespoons sugar
- 1 tablespoon cornstarch

Directions:

1. Insert the Cooking Pot and close the hood. Select GRILL, set the temperature to HI, and set the time to 20 minutes. Select START/STOP to begin preheating.
2. When the unit beeps to signify it has preheated, pour the water into the Cooking Pot and add the ramen noodles. Close the hood and cook for 5 minutes.
3. After 5 minutes, open the hood and remove the Cooking Pot. Drain the noodles and set aside. Insert the Grill Grate (along with the Cooking Pot). Make a large bed of noodles on the Grill Grate and drizzle olive oil over them. Close the hood and cook for 5 minutes. (If using chow mein noodles, flip them halfway through.)
4. After 5 minutes, the ramen noodles should be crispy and golden brown. Transfer the crispy noodles to a large serving plate.
5. Use grill mitts to remove the Grill Grate. To the Cooking Pot, add the remaining 3 tablespoons of olive oil and the garlic and ginger. Close the hood and cook for 2 minutes.
6. After 2 minutes, open the hood and add the red bell pepper, mushrooms, baby corn, snap peas, broccoli, and carrot. Close the hood and cook for 5 minutes.
7. While the vegetables are cooking, in a small bowl, combine the vegetable broth, soy sauce, vinegar, sesame oil, sugar, and cornstarch and mix until the sugar and cornstarch are dissolved.
8. After 5 minutes, open the hood, stir the vegetables, and add the broth mixture. Close the hood and cook for 3 minutes more.
9. When cooking is complete, open the hood and stir once more. Close the hood and let the vegetables sit in the pot for 3 minutes. Then, pour the vegetables and sauce on top of the crispy noodle bed and serve.

Zucchini And Onions Au Gratin

Servings: 4
Cooking Time: 15 Minutes
Ingredients:
- 1 cup panko bread crumbs
- 1 cup grated Parmesan cheese
- 1 large white onion, sliced
- 3 zucchini, cut into thin discs
- 1 teaspoon sea salt
- 1 teaspoon freshly ground black pepper
- 1 teaspoon onion powder
- 1 cup heavy (whipping) cream
- 1 tablespoon unsalted butter, at room temperature
- 1 teaspoon cornstarch

Directions:
1. Insert the Cooking Pot and close the hood. Select GRILL, set the temperature to MED, and set the time to 15 minutes. Select START/STOP to begin preheating.
2. While the unit is preheating, in a large bowl, combine the panko bread crumbs and Parmesan cheese.
3. When the unit beeps to signify it has preheated, add the onion to the Cooking Pot. Close the hood and cook for 2 minutes.
4. After 2 minutes, open the hood and add the zucchini, salt, pepper, and onion powder. Stir to mix. Close the hood and cook for 2 minutes.
5. After 2 minutes, open the hood and stir in the heavy cream, butter, and cornstarch. Close the hood and cook for 3 minutes.
6. After 3 minutes, the vegetable mixture should be creamy and thick. Evenly spread the bread crumb mixture over the top. Close the hood and cook for 8 minutes more.
7. When cooking is complete, the top will be golden brown and crunchy. Remove from the grill and serve.

Cheesy Macaroni Balls

Servings: 2
Cooking Time: 10 Minutes
Ingredients:
- 2 cups leftover macaroni
- 1 cup shredded Cheddar cheese
- ½ cup flour
- 1 cup bread crumbs
- 3 large eggs
- 1 cup milk
- ½ teaspoon salt
- ¼ teaspoon black pepper

Directions:
1. Insert the Crisper Basket and close the hood. Select AIR CRISP, set the temperature to 365ºF, and set the time to 10 minutes. Select START/STOP to begin preheating.
2. In a bowl, combine the leftover macaroni and shredded cheese.
3. Pour the flour in a separate bowl. Put the bread crumbs in a third bowl. Finally, in a fourth bowl, mix the eggs and milk with a whisk.
4. With an ice-cream scoop, create balls from the macaroni mixture. Coat them the flour, then in the egg mixture, and lastly in the bread crumbs.
5. Arrange the balls in the basket. Close the hood and AIR CRISP for 10 minutes, giving them an occasional stir. Ensure they crisp up nicely.
6. Serve hot.

Cheesy Asparagus And Potato Platter

Servings: 5
Cooking Time: 26 To 30 Minutes
Ingredients:

- 4 medium potatoes, cut into wedges
- Cooking spray
- 1 bunch asparagus, trimmed
- 2 tablespoons olive oil
- Salt and pepper, to taste
- Cheese Sauce:
- ¼ cup crumbled cottage cheese
- ¼ cup buttermilk
- 1 tablespoon whole-grain mustard
- Salt and black pepper, to taste

Directions:

1. Insert the Crisper Basket and close the hood. Select ROAST, set the temperature to 400ºF, and set the time to 30 minutes. Select START/STOP to begin preheating.
2. Spritz the Crisper Basket with cooking spray.
3. Put the potatoes in the Crisper Basket. Close the hood and ROAST for 20 to 22 minutes, until golden brown. Shake the basket halfway through the cooking time.
4. When ready, remove the potatoes from the basket to a platter. Cover the potatoes with foil to keep warm. Set aside.
5. Place the asparagus in the Crisper Basket and drizzle with the olive oil. Sprinkle with salt and pepper.
6. Close the hood and ROAST for 6 to 8 minutes, shaking the basket once or twice during cooking, or until the asparagus is cooked to your desired crispiness.
7. Meanwhile, make the cheese sauce by stirring together the cottage cheese, buttermilk, and mustard in a small bowl. Season with salt and pepper.
8. Transfer the asparagus to the platter of potatoes and drizzle with the cheese sauce. Serve immediately.

Fast And Easy Asparagus

Servings: 4
Cooking Time: 5 Minutes
Ingredients:

- 1 pound fresh asparagus spears, trimmed
- 1 tablespoon olive oil
- Salt and ground black pepper, to taste

Directions:

1. Insert the Crisper Basket and close the hood. Select AIR CRISP, set the temperature to 375ºF, and set the time to 5 minutes. Select START/STOP to begin preheating.
2. Combine all the ingredients and transfer to the Crisper Basket.
3. Close the hood and AIR CRISP for 5 minutes or until soft.
4. Serve hot.

Asian-inspired Broccoli

Servings: 2
Cooking Time: 10 Minutes
Ingredients:

- 12 ounces broccoli florets
- 2 tablespoons Asian hot chili oil
- 1 teaspoon ground Sichuan peppercorns (or black pepper)
- 2 garlic cloves, finely chopped
- 1 piece fresh ginger, peeled and finely chopped
- Kosher salt and freshly ground black pepper

Directions:

1. Insert the Crisper Basket and close the hood. Select ROAST, set the temperature to 375ºF, and set the time to 10 minutes. Select START/STOP to begin preheating.
2. Toss the broccoli florets with the chili oil, Sichuan peppercorns, garlic, ginger, salt, and pepper in a mixing bowl until thoroughly coated.
3. Transfer the broccoli florets to the Crisper Basket. Close the hood and ROAST for 10 minutes, shaking the basket halfway through, or until the broccoli florets are lightly browned and tender.
4. Remove the broccoli from the basket and serve on a plate.

Corn And Potato Chowder

Servings: 4
Cooking Time: 50 Minutes
Ingredients:

- 4 ears corn, shucked
- 2 tablespoons canola oil
- 1½ teaspoons sea salt, plus additional to season the corn
- ½ teaspoon freshly ground black pepper, plus additional to season the corn
- 3 tablespoons unsalted butter
- 1 small onion, finely chopped
- 2½ cups vegetable broth
- 1½ cups milk
- 4 cups diced potatoes
- 2 cups half-and-half
- 1½ teaspoons chopped fresh thyme

Directions:

1. Insert the Grill Grate and close the hood. Select GRILL, set the temperature to MAX, and set the time to 12 minutes. Select START/STOP to begin preheating.
2. While the unit is preheating, brush each ear of corn with ½ tablespoon of oil. Season the corn with salt and pepper to taste.
3. When the unit beeps to signify it has preheated, place the corn on the Grill Grate and close the hood. GRILL for 6 minutes.
4. After 6 minutes, flip the corn. Close the hood and continue cooking for the remaining 6 minutes.
5. When cooking is complete, remove the corn and let cool. Cut the kernels from the cobs.
6. In a food processor, purée 1 cup of corn kernels until smooth.
7. In a large pot over medium-high heat, melt the butter. Add the onion and sauté until soft, 5 to 7 minutes. Add the broth, milk, and potatoes. Bring to a simmer and cook until the potatoes are just tender, 10 to 12 minutes. Stir in the salt and pepper.
8. Stir in the puréed corn, remaining corn kernels, and half-and-half. Bring to a simmer and cook, stirring occasionally, until the potatoes are cooked through, for 15 to 20 minutes.
9. Using a potato masher or immersion blender, slightly mash some of the potatoes. Stir in the thyme, and additional salt and pepper to taste.

Sesame-thyme Whole Maitake Mushrooms

Servings: 2
Cooking Time: 15 Minutes
Ingredients:

- 1 tablespoon soy sauce
- 2 teaspoons toasted sesame oil
- 3 teaspoons vegetable oil, divided
- 1 garlic clove, minced
- 7 ounces maitake (hen of the woods) mushrooms
- ½ teaspoon flaky sea salt
- ½ teaspoon sesame seeds
- ½ teaspoon finely chopped fresh thyme leaves

Directions:

1. Insert the Crisper Basket and close the hood. Select ROAST, set the temperature to 300ºF, and set the time to 15 minutes. Select START/STOP to begin preheating.
2. Whisk together the soy sauce, sesame oil, 1 teaspoon of vegetable oil, and garlic in a small bowl.
3. Arrange the mushrooms in the Crisper Basket in a single layer. Drizzle the soy sauce mixture over the mushrooms. Close the hood and ROAST for 10 minutes.
4. Flip the mushrooms and sprinkle the sea salt, sesame seeds, and thyme leaves on top. Drizzle the remaining 2 teaspoons of vegetable oil all over. Roast for an additional 5 minutes.
5. Remove the mushrooms from the basket to a plate and serve hot.

Arugula And Broccoli Salad

Servings: 4
Cooking Time: 12 Minutes
Ingredients:

- 2 heads broccoli, trimmed into florets
- ½ red onion, sliced
- 1 tablespoon canola oil
- 2 tablespoons extra-virgin olive oil
- 1 tablespoon freshly squeezed lemon juice
- 1 teaspoon honey
- 1 teaspoon Dijon mustard
- 1 garlic clove, minced
- Pinch red pepper flakes
- ¼ teaspoon fine sea salt
- Freshly ground black pepper, to taste
- 4 cups arugula, torn
- 2 tablespoons grated Parmesan cheese

Directions:

1. Insert the Grill Grate and close the hood. Select GRILL, set the temperature to MAX, and set the time to 12 minutes. Select START/STOP to begin preheating.
2. While the unit is preheating, in a large bowl, combine the broccoli, sliced onions, and canola oil and toss until coated.
3. When the unit beeps to signify it has preheated, place the vegetables on the Grill Grate. Close the hood and GRILL for 8 to 12 minutes, until charred on all sides.
4. Meanwhile, in a medium bowl, whisk together the olive oil, lemon juice, honey, mustard, garlic, red pepper flakes, salt, and pepper.
5. When cooking is complete, combine the roasted vegetables and arugula in a large serving bowl. Drizzle with the vinaigrette, and sprinkle with the Parmesan cheese.

Grilled Mozzarella Eggplant Stacks

Servings: 4
Cooking Time: 14 Minutes
Ingredients:

- 1 eggplant, sliced ¼-inch thick
- 2 tablespoons canola oil
- 2 beefsteak or heirloom tomatoes, sliced ¼-inch thick
- 12 large basil leaves
- ½ pound buffalo Mozzarella, sliced ¼-inch thick
- Sea salt, to taste

Directions:

1. Insert the Grill Grate and close the hood. Select GRILL, set the temperature to MAX, and set the time to 14 minutes. Select START/STOP to begin preheating.
2. Meanwhile, in a large bowl, toss the eggplant and oil until evenly coated.
3. When the unit beeps to signify it has preheated, place the eggplant on the Grill Grate. Close the hood and GRILL for 8 to 12 minutes, until charred on all sides.
4. After 8 to 12 minutes, top the eggplant with one slice each of tomato and Mozzarella. Close the hood and GRILL for 2 minutes, until the cheese melts.
5. When cooking is complete, remove the eggplant stacks from the grill. Place 2 or 3 basil leaves on top of half of the stacks. Place the remaining eggplant stacks on top of those with basil so that there are four stacks total. Season with salt, garnish with the remaining basil, and serve.

Creamy Corn Casserole

Servings: 4
Cooking Time: 15 Minutes
Ingredients:

- 2 cups frozen yellow corn
- 1 egg, beaten
- 3 tablespoons flour
- ½ cup grated Swiss or Havarti cheese
- ½ cup light cream
- ¼ cup milk
- Pinch salt
- Freshly ground black pepper, to taste
- 2 tablespoons butter, cut into cubes
- Nonstick cooking spray

Directions:
1. Select BAKE, set the temperature to 320ºF, and set the time to 15 minutes. Select START/STOP to begin preheating.
2. Spritz a baking pan with nonstick cooking spray.
3. Stir together the remaining ingredients except the butter in a medium bowl until well incorporated.
4. Transfer the mixture to the prepared baking pan and scatter with the butter cubes.
5. Place the pan directly in the pot. Close the hood and BAKE for 15 minutes, or until the top is golden brown and a toothpick inserted in the center comes out clean.
6. Let the casserole cool for 5 minutes before slicing into wedges and serving.

Grilled Mozzarella And Tomatoes

Servings: 4
Cooking Time: 5 Minutes
Ingredients:

- 4 large, round, firm tomatoes
- ½ cup Italian dressing
- 1 cup shredded mozzarella
- ½ cup chopped fresh basil, for garnish

Directions:
1. Insert the Grill Grate and close the hood. Select GRILL, set the temperature to HI, and set the time to 5 minutes. Select START/STOP to begin preheating.
2. While the unit is preheating, cut the tomatoes in half crosswise. Pour about 1 tablespoon of Italian dressing on each tomato half.
3. When the unit beeps to signify it has preheated, place the tomatoes on the Grill Grate, cut-side up. If the tomatoes won't stand upright, slice a small piece from the bottom to level them out. Close the hood and grill for 2 minutes.
4. After 2 minutes, open the hood and evenly distribute the mozzarella cheese on top of the tomatoes. Close the hood and cook for 3 minutes more, or until the cheese is melted.
5. When cooking is complete, remove the tomatoes from the grill. Garnish with the basil and serve.

Sweet Pepper Poppers

Servings: 4
Cooking Time: 7 Minutes
Ingredients:

- 10 mini sweet peppers
- ½ cup mayonnaise
- 1 cup shredded sharp cheddar cheese
- ½ teaspoon onion powder
- ⅛ teaspoon cayenne powder (optional)

Directions:
1. Insert the Grill Grate and close the hood. Select GRILL, set the temperature to HI, and set the time to 7 minutes. Select START/STOP to begin preheating.
2. While the unit is preheating, cut the peppers in half lengthwise and scoop out the seeds and membranes. In a small bowl, combine the mayonnaise, cheddar cheese, onion powder, and cayenne powder (if using). Spoon the cheese mixture into each sweet pepper half.
3. When the unit beeps to signify it has preheated, place the sweet peppers on the Grill Grate, cut-side up. Close the hood and grill for 7 minutes.
4. When cooking is complete, remove the peppers from the grill and serve. Or if you prefer your peppers more charred, continue cooking to your liking.

Bean And Corn Stuffed Peppers

Servings: 6
Cooking Time: 32 Minutes
Ingredients:

- 6 red or green bell peppers, seeded, ribs removed, and top ½-inch cut off and reserved
- 4 garlic cloves, minced
- 1 small white onion, diced
- 2 bags instant rice, cooked in microwave
- 1 can red or green enchilada sauce
- ½ teaspoon chili powder
- ¼ teaspoon ground cumin
- ½ cup canned black beans, rinsed and drained
- ½ cup frozen corn
- ½ cup vegetable stock
- 1 bag shredded Colby Jack cheese, divided

Directions:

1. Chop the ½-inch portions of reserved bell pepper and place in a large mixing bowl. Add the garlic, onion, cooked instant rice, enchilada sauce, chili powder, cumin, black beans, corn, vegetable stock, and half the cheese. Mix to combine.
2. Use the cooking pot without the Grill Grate or Crisper Basket installed. Close the hood. Select ROAST, set the temperature to 350°F, and set the time to 32 minutes. Select START/STOP to begin preheating.
3. While the unit is preheating, spoon the mixture into the peppers, filling them up as full as possible. If necessary, lightly press the mixture down into the peppers to fit more in.
4. When the unit beeps to signify it has preheated, place the peppers, upright, in the pot. Close the hood and ROAST for 30 minutes.
5. After 30 minutes, sprinkle the remaining cheese over the top of the peppers. Close the hood and ROAST for the remaining 2 minutes.
6. When cooking is complete, serve immediately.

Flatbread Pizza

Servings: 4
Cooking Time: 10 Minutes
Ingredients:

- 1 (14-ounce) package refrigerated pizza dough
- 2 tablespoons extra-virgin olive oil
- ½ cup prepared Alfredo sauce
- 1 medium zucchini, cut into ⅛-inch-thick discs
- ½ cup fresh spinach
- ½ red onion, sliced
- 4 cherry tomatoes, sliced

Directions:

1. Insert the Grill Grate and close the hood. Select GRILL, set the temperature to MED, and set the time to 10 minutes. Select START/STOP to begin preheating.
2. While the unit is preheating, roll out the dough into a rectangle slightly smaller than the Grill Grate (8 by 11 inches). Brush the olive oil on both sides of the dough.
3. When the unit beeps to signify it has preheated, place the dough on the Grill Grate. Close the hood and grill for 5 minutes.
4. After 5 minutes, open the hood and flip the dough. (Or skip flipping, if you'd rather.) Spread the Alfredo sauce across the dough, leaving a 1-inch border. Layer the zucchini, spinach, red onion, and cherry tomatoes across the dough. Close the hood and cook for 5 minutes more.
5. When cooking is complete, remove the pizza from the grill. Slice and serve.

Mozzarella Broccoli Calzones

Servings: 4

Cooking Time: 24 Minutes

Ingredients:

- 1 head broccoli, trimmed into florets
- 2 tablespoons extra-virgin olive oil
- 1 store-bought pizza dough
- 2 to 3 tablespoons all-purpose flour, plus more for dusting
- 1 egg, beaten
- 2 cups shredded Mozzarella cheese
- 1 cup ricotta cheese
- ½ cup grated Parmesan cheese
- 1 garlic clove, grated
- Grated zest of 1 lemon
- ½ teaspoon red pepper flakes
- Cooking oil spray

Directions:

1. Insert the Crisper Basket and close the hood. Select AIR CRISP, set the temperature to 390°F, and set the time to 12 minutes. Select START/STOP to begin preheating.

2. Meanwhile, in a large bowl, toss the broccoli and olive oil until evenly coated.

3. When the unit beeps to signify it has preheated, add the broccoli to the basket. Close the hood and AIR CRISP for 6 minutes.

4. While the broccoli is cooking, divide the pizza dough into four equal pieces. Dust a clean work surface with the flour. Place the dough on the floured surface and roll each piece into an 8-inch round of even thickness. Dust your rolling pin and work surface with additional flour, as needed, to ensure the dough does not stick. Brush a thin coating of egg wash around the edges of each round.

5. After 6 minutes, shake the basket of broccoli. Place the basket back in the unit and close the hood to resume cooking.

6. Meanwhile, in a medium bowl, combine the Mozzarella, ricotta, Parmesan cheese, garlic, lemon zest, and red pepper flakes.

7. After cooking is complete, add the broccoli to the cheese mixture. Spoon one-quarter of the mixture onto one side of each dough. Fold the other half over the filling, and press firmly to seal the edges together. Brush each calzone all over with the remaining egg wash.

8. Select AIR CRISP, set the temperature to 390°F, and set the time to 12 minutes. Select START/STOP to begin preheating.

9. When the unit beeps to signify it has preheated, coat the Crisper Basket with cooking spray and place the calzones in the basket. AIR CRISP for 10 to 12 minutes, until golden brown.

Green Beans With Sun-dried Tomatoes And Feta

Servings: 8
Cooking Time: 8 Minutes
Ingredients:

- 2 pounds green beans, ends trimmed
- 2 tablespoons extra-virgin olive oil
- 1 teaspoon salt
- ½ teaspoon freshly ground black pepper
- 1 cup sun-dried tomatoes packed in oil, undrained, sliced
- 6 ounces feta cheese, crumbled

Directions:

1. Insert the Grill Grate and close the hood. Select GRILL, set the temperature to HI, and set the time to 8 minutes. Select START/STOP to begin preheating.
2. While the unit is preheating, in a large bowl, toss the green beans with the olive oil, salt, and pepper.
3. When the unit beeps to signify it has preheated, place the green beans on the Grill Grate. Close the hood and grill for 4 minutes.
4. After 4 minutes, open the hood and flip the green beans. Close the hood and cook for 4 minutes more.
5. When cooking is complete, transfer the green beans to a large bowl. Add the sun-dried tomatoes and mix together. Top with the feta cheese and serve.

Garlic Roasted Asparagus

Servings: 4
Cooking Time: 10 Minutes
Ingredients:

- 1 pound asparagus, woody ends trimmed
- 2 tablespoons olive oil
- 1 tablespoon balsamic vinegar
- 2 teaspoons minced garlic
- Salt and freshly ground black pepper, to taste

Directions:

1. Insert the Crisper Basket and close the hood. Select ROAST, set the temperature to 400ºF, and set the time to 10 minutes. Select START/STOP to begin preheating.
2. In a large shallow bowl, toss the asparagus with the olive oil, balsamic vinegar, garlic, salt, and pepper until thoroughly coated.
3. Arrange the asparagus in the Crisper Basket. Close the hood and ROAST for 10 minutes until crispy. Flip the asparagus with tongs halfway through the cooking time.
4. Serve warm.

Desserts

Banana And Walnut Cake

Servings: 6
Cooking Time: 25 Minutes
Ingredients:

- 1 pound bananas, mashed
- 8 ounces flour
- 6 ounces sugar
- 3.5 ounces walnuts, chopped
- 2.5 ounces butter, melted
- 2 eggs, lightly beaten
- ¼ teaspoon baking soda

Directions:
1. Select BAKE, set the temperature to 355ºF, and set the time to 10 minutes. Select START/STOP to begin preheating.
2. In a bowl, combine the sugar, butter, egg, flour, and baking soda with a whisk. Stir in the bananas and walnuts.
3. Transfer the mixture to a greased baking pan. Place the pan directly in the pot. Close the hood and BAKE for 10 minutes.
4. Reduce the temperature to 330ºF and bake for another 15 minutes. Serve hot.

Chocolate And Peanut Butter Lava Cupcakes

Servings: 8
Cooking Time: 10 To 13 Minutes
Ingredients:

- Nonstick baking spray with flour
- 1⅓ cups chocolate cake mix
- 1 egg
- 1 egg yolk
- ¼ cup safflower oil
- ¼ cup hot water
- ⅓ cup sour cream
- 3 tablespoons peanut butter
- 1 tablespoon powdered sugar

Directions:
1. Select BAKE, set the temperature to 350ºF, and set the time to 13 minutes. Select START/STOP to begin preheating.
2. Double up 16 foil muffin cups to make 8 cups. Spray each lightly with nonstick spray; set aside.
3. In a medium bowl, combine the cake mix, egg, egg yolk, safflower oil, water, and sour cream, and beat until combined.
4. In a small bowl, combine the peanut butter and powdered sugar and mix well. Form this mixture into 8 balls.
5. Spoon about ¼ cup of the chocolate batter into each muffin cup and top with a peanut butter ball. Spoon remaining batter on top of the peanut butter balls to cover them.
6. Arrange the cups in the pot, leaving some space between each. Place the pan directly in the pot. Close the hood and BAKE for 10 to 13 minutes or until the tops look dry and set.
7. Let the cupcakes cool for about 10 minutes, then serve warm.

Marshmallow Banana Boat

Servings: 4
Cooking Time: 6 Minutes
Ingredients:

- 4 ripe bananas
- 1 cup mini marshmallows
- ½ cup chocolate chips
- ½ cup peanut butter chips

Directions:
1. Insert the Grill Grate and close the hood. Select GRILL, set the temperature to MEDIUM, and set the time to 6 minutes. Select START/STOP to begin preheating.
2. While the unit is preheating, slice each banana lengthwise while still in its peel, making sure not to cut all the way through. Using both hands, pull the banana peel open like you would a book, revealing the banana inside. Divide the marshmallows, chocolate chips, and peanut butter chips among the bananas, stuffing them inside the skin.
3. When the unit beeps to signify it has preheated, place the stuffed banana on the Grill Grate. Close the hood and GRILL for 4 to 6 minutes, until the chocolate is melted and the marshmallows are toasted.

Chocolate Pecan Pie

Servings: 8
Cooking Time: 25 Minutes
Ingredients:
- 1 unbaked pie crust
- Filling:
- 2 large eggs
- ⅓ cup butter, melted
- 1 cup sugar
- ½ cup all-purpose flour
- 1 cup milk chocolate chips
- 1½ cups coarsely chopped pecans
- 2 tablespoons bourbon

Directions:
1. Select BAKE, set the temperature to 350ºF, and set the time to 25 minutes. Select START/STOP to begin preheating.
2. Whisk the eggs and melted butter in a large bowl until creamy.
3. Add the sugar and flour and stir to incorporate. Mix in the milk chocolate chips, pecans, and bourbon and stir until well combined.
4. Use a fork to prick holes in the bottom and sides of the pie crust. Pour the prepared filling into the pie crust. Place the pie crust in the pot.
5. Close the hood and BAKE for 25 minutes until a toothpick inserted in the center comes out clean.
6. Allow the pie cool for 10 minutes in the basket before serving.

Mini Brownie Cakes

Servings:4
Cooking Time: 15 Minutes
Ingredients:
- 8 tablespoons (1 stick) unsalted butter
- 2 large eggs
- ¼ cup unsweetened cocoa powder
- ½ cup granulated sugar
- ½ teaspoon vanilla extract
- ⅛ teaspoon salt
- ½ cup all-purpose flour

Directions:
1. Cut the butter into quarters and divide them between 2 (6-ounce) ramekins. Insert the Cooking Pot, place the ramekins in the pot, and close the hood. Select GRILL, set the temperature to LO, and set the time to 15 minutes. Select START/STOP to begin preheating. After 3 minutes of preheating (set a separate timer), use grill mitts to remove the ramekins and set aside. Close the hood to continue preheating.
2. While the unit is preheating, in a large bowl, whisk the eggs together, then add the cocoa powder, sugar, vanilla, and salt. Sift or gradually shake the flour into the bowl as you continue mixing. Then stir in the melted butter to form a smooth batter. Divide the batter evenly among 4 (6-ounce) ramekins, filling them no more than three-quarters full.
3. When the unit beeps to signify it has preheated, place the ramekins in the Cooking Pot. Close the hood and cook for 15 minutes.
4. When cooking is complete, open the hood and remove the ramekins. The brownies are done when a toothpick inserted in the center comes out clean. (Cooking them for 15 minutes usually gives the brownies a crispy crust with a fudgy center. Add another 3 to 5 minutes if you wish to cook the center all the way through.)

Cinnamon Candied Apples

Servings: 4
Cooking Time: 12 Minutes
Ingredients:
- 1 cup packed light brown sugar
- 2 teaspoons ground cinnamon
- 2 medium Granny Smith apples, peeled and diced

Directions:
1. Select BAKE, set the temperature to 350ºF, and set the time to 12 minutes. Select START/STOP to begin preheating.
2. Thoroughly combine the brown sugar and cinnamon in a medium bowl.
3. Add the apples to the bowl and stir until well coated. Transfer the apples to a baking pan.
4. Place the pan directly in the pot. Close the hood and BAKE for 9 minutes. Stir the apples once and bake for an additional 3 minutes until softened.
5. Serve warm.

Curry Peaches, Pears, And Plums

Servings: 6 To 8
Cooking Time: 5 Minutes
Ingredients:
- 2 peaches
- 2 firm pears
- 2 plums
- 2 tablespoons melted butter
- 1 tablespoon honey
- 2 to 3 teaspoons curry powder

Directions:
1. Insert the Crisper Basket and close the hood. Select BAKE, set the temperature to 325ºF, and set the time to 8 minutes. Select START/STOP to begin preheating.
2. Cut the peaches in half, remove the pits, and cut each half in half again. Cut the pears in half, core them, and remove the stem. Cut each half in half again. Do the same with the plums.
3. Spread a large sheet of heavy-duty foil on the work surface. Arrange the fruit on the foil and drizzle with the butter and honey. Sprinkle with the curry powder.
4. Wrap the fruit in the foil, making sure to leave some air space in the packet.
5. Put the foil package in the basket. Close the hood and BAKE for 5 to 8 minutes, shaking the basket once during the cooking time, until the fruit is soft.
6. Serve immediately.

Cinnamon-sugar Dessert Chips

Servings: 4
Cooking Time: 10 Minutes
Ingredients:
- 10 (6-inch) flour tortillas
- 8 tablespoons (1 stick) unsalted butter, melted
- 1 tablespoon cinnamon
- ¼ cup granulated sugar
- ½ cup chocolate syrup, for dipping

Directions:
1. Insert the Grill Grate and close the hood. Select GRILL, set the temperature to HI, and set the time to 10 minutes. Select START/STOP to begin preheating.
2. While the unit is preheating, cut the tortillas into 6 equal wedges. In a large resealable bag, combine the tortillas, butter, cinnamon, and sugar and shake vigorously to coat the tortillas.
3. When the unit beeps to signify it has preheated, add half the tortillas to the Grill Grate. Close the hood and cook for 2 minutes, 30 seconds.
4. After 2 minutes, 30 seconds, open the hood and use a spatula to quickly flip the chips or move them around. Close the hood and cook for 2 minutes, 30 seconds more.
5. After 2 minutes, 30 seconds, open the hood and remove the grilled chips and repeat the process with the remaining tortillas.
6. Serve with the chocolate syrup for dipping.

Strawberry Pizza

Servings: 4
Cooking Time: 6 Minutes
Ingredients:

- 2 tablespoons all-purpose flour, plus more as needed
- ½ store-bought pizza dough
- 1 tablespoon canola oil
- 1 cup sliced fresh strawberries
- 1 tablespoon sugar
- ½ cup chocolate-hazelnut spread

Directions:

1. Insert the Grill Grate and close the hood. Select GRILL, set the temperature to MAX, and set the time to 6 minutes. Select START/STOP to begin preheating.
2. While the unit is preheating, dust a clean work surface with the flour. Place the dough on the floured surface, and roll it out to a 9-inch round of even thickness. Dust your rolling pin and work surface with additional flour, as needed, to ensure the dough does not stick.
3. Brush the surface of the rolled-out dough evenly with half the oil. Flip the dough over, and brush with the remaining oil. Poke the dough with a fork 5 or 6 times across its surface to prevent air pockets from forming during cooking.
4. When the unit beeps to signify it has preheated, place the dough on the Grill Grate. Close the hood and GRILL for 3 minutes.
5. After 3 minutes, flip the dough. Close the hood and continue grilling for the remaining 3 minutes.
6. Meanwhile, in a medium mixing bowl, combine the strawberries and sugar.
7. Transfer the pizza to a cutting board and let cool. Top with the chocolate-hazelnut spread and strawberries. Cut into pieces and serve.

Chocolate S'mores

Servings: 12
Cooking Time: 3 Minutes
Ingredients:

- 12 whole cinnamon graham crackers
- 2 chocolate bars, broken into 12 pieces
- 12 marshmallows

Directions:

1. Insert the Crisper Basket and close the hood. Select BAKE, set the temperature to 350ºF, and set the time to 3 minutes. Select START/STOP to begin preheating.
2. Halve each graham cracker into 2 squares.
3. Put 6 graham cracker squares in the basket. Do not stack. Put a piece of chocolate into each. Close the hood and BAKE for 2 minutes.
4. Open the grill and add a marshmallow onto each piece of melted chocolate. Bake for 1 additional minute.
5. Remove the cooked s'mores from the grill, then repeat steps 2 and 3 for the remaining 6 s'mores.
6. Top with the remaining graham cracker squares and serve.

Rich Chocolate Cookie

Servings: 4
Cooking Time: 9 Minutes
Ingredients:
- Nonstick baking spray with flour
- 3 tablespoons softened butter
- ⅓ cup plus 1 tablespoon brown sugar
- 1 egg yolk
- ½ cup flour
- 2 tablespoons ground white chocolate
- ¼ teaspoon baking soda
- ½ teaspoon vanilla
- ¾ cup chocolate chips

Directions:
1. Select BAKE, set the temperature to 350ºF, and set the time to 9 minutes. Select START/STOP to begin preheating.
2. In a medium bowl, beat the butter and brown sugar together until fluffy. Stir in the egg yolk.
3. Add the flour, white chocolate, baking soda, and vanilla, and mix well. Stir in the chocolate chips.
4. Line a baking pan with parchment paper. Spray the parchment paper with nonstick baking spray with flour.
5. Spread the batter into the prepared pan, leaving a ½-inch border on all sides.
6. Place the pan directly in the pot. Close the hood and BAKE for 9 minutes or until the cookie is light brown and just barely set.
7. Remove the pan from the grill and let cool for 10 minutes. Remove the cookie from the pan, remove the parchment paper, and let cool on a wire rack.
8. Serve immediately.

Grilled Peaches With Bourbon Butter Sauce

Servings: 4
Cooking Time: 12 Minutes
Ingredients:
- 4 tablespoons salted butter
- ¼ cup bourbon
- ½ cup brown sugar
- 4 ripe peaches, halved and pitted
- ¼ cup candied pecans

Directions:
1. Insert the Grill Grate and close the hood. Select GRILL, set the temperature to MAX, and set the time to 12 minutes. Select START/STOP to begin preheating.
2. While the unit is preheating, in a saucepan over medium heat, melt the butter for about 5 minutes. Once the butter is browned, remove the pan from the heat and carefully add the bourbon.
3. Return the saucepan to medium-high heat and add the brown sugar. Bring to a boil and let the sugar dissolve for 5 minutes stirring occasionally.
4. Pour the bourbon butter sauce into a medium shallow bowl and arrange the peaches cut-side down to coat in the sauce.
5. When the unit beeps to signify it has preheated, place the fruit on the Grill Grate in a single layer (you may need to do this in multiple batches). Gently press the fruit down to maximize grill marks. Close the hood and GRILL for 10 to 12 minutes without flipping. If working in batches, repeat this step for all the peaches.
6. When cooking is complete, remove the peaches and top each with the pecans. Drizzle with the remaining bourbon butter sauce and serve immediately.

Everyday Cheesecake

Servings: 4
Cooking Time: 35 Minutes
Ingredients:

- 1 large egg
- 8 ounces cream cheese, at room temperature
- ¼ cup heavy (whipping) cream
- ¼ cup sour cream
- ¼ cup powdered sugar
- 1 teaspoon vanilla extract
- 5 ounces cookies, such as chocolate, vanilla, cinnamon, or your favorite
- 4 tablespoons (½ stick) unsalted butter, melted

Directions:

1. In a large bowl, whisk the egg. Then add the cream cheese, heavy cream, and sour cream and whisk until smooth. Slowly add the powdered sugar and vanilla, whisking until fully mixed.
2. Insert the Cooking Pot and close the hood. Select BAKE, set the temperature to 350°F, and set the time to 35 minutes. Select START/STOP to begin preheating.
3. While the unit is preheating, crush the cookies into fine crumbs. Place them in a 6-inch springform pan and drizzle evenly with the melted butter. Using your fingers, press down on the crumbs to form a crust on the bottom of the pan. Pour the cream cheese mixture on top of the crust. Cover the pan with aluminum foil, making sure the foil fully covers the sides of the pan and tucks under the bottom so it does not lift up and block the Splatter Shield as the air flows while baking.
4. When the unit beeps to signify it has preheated, place the springform pan in the Cooking Pot. Close the hood and cook for 25 minutes.
5. After 25 minutes, open the hood and remove the foil. Close the hood and cook for 10 minutes more.
6. When cooking is complete, remove the pan from the Cooking Pot and let the cheesecake cool for 1 hour, then place the cheesecake in the refrigerator for at least 3 hours. Slice and serve.

Biscuit Raisin Bread

Servings: 6 To 8
Cooking Time: 20 Minutes
Ingredients:

- 1 (12-ounce) package refrigerated buttermilk biscuits (10 biscuits)
- 8 ounces cream cheese, cut into 40 cubes
- ¼ cup light brown sugar, packed
- 4 tablespoons (½ stick) unsalted butter, melted
- ½ cup raisins

Directions:

1. Insert the Cooking Pot and close the hood. Select GRILL, set the temperature to LO, and set the time to 20 minutes. Select START/STOP to begin preheating.
2. While the unit is preheating, separate the biscuits and cut each into quarters. Flatten each quarter biscuit with your palm and place 1 cream cheese cube on the center. Wrap the dough around the cream cheese and press to seal, forming a ball. Place the biscuit balls in a 9-by-5-inch bread loaf pan. They will be layered over each other.
3. In a small bowl, combine the brown sugar and melted butter. Pour this over the biscuit balls evenly.
4. When the unit beeps to signify it has preheated, place the loaf pan in the Cooking Pot. Close the hood and grill for 10 minutes.
5. After 10 minutes, open the hood and evenly scatter the raisins on the top layer. Close the hood and cook for 10 minutes more.
6. When cooking is complete, remove the loaf pan from the pot. Remove the bread from the pan, slice, and serve.

Peaches-and-cake Skewers

Servings: 4
Cooking Time: 8 Minutes
Ingredients:

- 1 loaf pound cake, cut into 1-inch cubes
- 4 peaches, sliced
- ½ cup condensed milk

Directions:

1. Insert the Grill Grate and close the hood. Select GRILL, set the temperature to HI, and set the time to 8 minutes. Select START/STOP to begin preheating.
2. While the unit is preheating, alternate cake cubes and peach slices, 3 or 4 pieces of each, on each of 12 skewers. Using a basting brush, brush the condensed milk onto the cake and peaches and place the skewers on a plate or baking sheet.
3. When the unit beeps to signify it has preheated, place 6 skewers on the Grill Grate. Close the hood and cook for 2 minutes.
4. After 2 minutes, open the hood and flip the skewers. Close the hood to cook for 2 minutes more.
5. After 2 minutes, open the hood and remove the skewers. Repeat steps 3 and 4 with the remaining 6 skewers. Serve.

Sweet Potato Donuts

Servings:12
Cooking Time: 52 Minutes
Ingredients:

- 3 cups water
- 1 medium white sweet potato
- ⅔ cup all-purpose flour, plus more for dusting
- ½ cup granulated sugar
- Avocado oil

Directions:

1. Insert the Cooking Pot, pour in the water, and close the hood. Select BROIL, set the temperature to 500°F, and set the time to 20 minutes. Select START/STOP to begin preheating.
2. While the unit is preheating, peel the sweet potato and cut it into chunks.
3. When the unit beeps to signify it has preheated, add the sweet potato to the Cooking Pot, making sure the chunks are fully submerged in the water. Close the hood and cook for 20 minutes.
4. After 20 minutes, open the hood and pierce a potato chunk to check for doneness—it should be easy to slice into. Remove and drain the sweet potatoes.
5. In a large bowl, mash the sweet potato with a masher or fork. When it has cooled down, add ⅔ cup of flour and the sugar and mix until well combined. The dough will be sticky. Dust a clean work surface with some flour. Roll and knead the dough until it is no longer sticky and holds its form, using more flour as needed.
6. Divide the dough in half and then cut each half into 6 equal-size pieces. Roll each piece of dough into a cylinder about 4 inches long.
7. Insert the Cooking Pot and close the hood. Select GRILL, set the temperature to HI, and set the time to 16 minutes. Select START/STOP to begin preheating.
8. While the unit is preheating, brush avocado oil on a 6-ring donut pan and place 6 donuts in the molds. Brush more avocado oil on top.
9. When the unit beeps to signify it has preheated, place the donut pan in the Cooking Pot. Close the hood and grill for 8 minutes.
10. When cooking is complete, remove the pan and transfer the donuts to a rack to cool.
11. Repeat steps 8 through 10 with the remaining donuts. Serve.

Ultimate Coconut Chocolate Cake

Servings: 10
Cooking Time: 15 Minutes
Ingredients:

- 1¼ cups unsweetened bakers' chocolate
- 1 stick butter
- 1 teaspoon liquid stevia
- ⅓ cup shredded coconut
- 2 tablespoons coconut milk
- 2 eggs, beaten
- Cooking spray

Directions:

1. Select BAKE, set the temperature to 330ºF, and set the time to 15 minutes. Select START/STOP to begin preheating.
2. Lightly spritz a baking pan with cooking spray.
3. Place the chocolate, butter, and stevia in a microwave-safe bowl. Microwave for about 30 seconds until melted. Let the chocolate mixture cool to room temperature.
4. Add the remaining ingredients to the chocolate mixture and stir until well incorporated. Pour the batter into the prepared baking pan.
5. Place the pan directly in the pot. Close the hood and BAKE for 15 minutes, or until a toothpick inserted in the center comes out clean.
6. Remove from the pan and allow to cool for about 10 minutes before serving.

Orange Coconut Cake

Servings: 6
Cooking Time: 17 Minutes
Ingredients:

- 1 stick butter, melted
- ¾ cup granulated Swerve
- 2 eggs, beaten
- ¾ cup coconut flour
- ¼ teaspoon salt
- ⅓ teaspoon grated nutmeg
- ⅓ cup coconut milk
- 1¼ cups almond flour
- ½ teaspoon baking powder
- 2 tablespoons unsweetened orange jam
- Cooking spray

Directions:

1. Select BAKE, set the temperature to 355ºF, and set the time to 17 minutes. Select START/STOP to begin preheating.
2. Coat a baking pan with cooking spray. Set aside.
3. In a large mixing bowl, whisk together the melted butter and granulated Swerve until fluffy.
4. Mix in the beaten eggs and whisk again until smooth. Stir in the coconut flour, salt, and nutmeg and gradually pour in the coconut milk. Add the remaining ingredients and stir until well incorporated.
5. Scrape the batter into the baking pan.
6. Place the pan directly in the pot. Close the hood and BAKE for 17 minutes until the top of the cake springs back when gently pressed with your fingers.
7. Remove from the grill to a wire rack to cool. Serve chilled.

Rum Grilled Pineapple Sundaes

Servings: 6
Cooking Time: 8 Minutes
Ingredients:

- ½ cup dark rum
- ½ cup packed brown sugar
- 1 teaspoon ground cinnamon, plus more for garnish
- 1 pineapple, cored and sliced
- Vanilla ice cream, for serving

Directions:

1. In a large shallow bowl or storage container, combine the rum, sugar, and cinnamon. Add the pineapple slices and arrange them in a single layer. Coat with the mixture, then let soak for at least 5 minutes per side.
2. Insert the Grill Grate and close the hood. Select GRILL, set the temperature to MAX, and set the time to 8 minutes. Select START/STOP to begin preheating.
3. While the unit is preheating, strain the extra rum sauce from the pineapple.
4. When the unit beeps to signify it has preheated, place the fruit on the Grill Grate in a single layer (you may need to do this in multiple batches). Gently press the fruit down to maximize grill marks. Close the hood and GRILL for about 6 to 8 minutes without flipping. If working in batches, remove the pineapple, and repeat this step for the remaining pineapple slices.
5. When cooking is complete, remove, and top each pineapple ring with a scoop of ice cream. Sprinkle with cinnamon and serve immediately.

Graham Cracker Cheesecake

Servings: 8
Cooking Time: 20 Minutes
Ingredients:

- 1 cup graham cracker crumbs
- 3 tablespoons softened butter
- 1½ packages cream cheese, softened
- ⅓ cup sugar
- 2 eggs
- 1 tablespoon flour
- 1 teaspoon vanilla
- ¼ cup chocolate syrup

Directions:

1. For the crust, combine the graham cracker crumbs and butter in a small bowl and mix well. Press into the bottom of a baking pan and put in the freezer to set.
2. For the filling, combine the cream cheese and sugar in a medium bowl and mix well. Beat in the eggs, one at a time. Add the flour and vanilla.
3. Select BAKE, set the temperature to 450ºF, and set the time to 20 minutes. Select START/STOP to begin preheating.
4. Remove ⅔ cup of the filling to a small bowl and stir in the chocolate syrup until combined.
5. Pour the vanilla filling into the pan with the crust. Drop the chocolate filling over the vanilla filling by the spoonful. With a clean butter knife, stir the fillings in a zigzag pattern to marbleize them.
6. Place the pan directly in the pot. Close the hood and BAKE for 20 minutes or until the cheesecake is just set.
7. Cool on a wire rack for 1 hour, then chill in the refrigerator until the cheesecake is firm.
8. Serve immediately.

Chocolate Molten Cake

Servings: 4
Cooking Time: 10 Minutes
Ingredients:

- 3.5 ounces butter, melted
- 3½ tablespoons sugar
- 3.5 ounces chocolate, melted
- 1½ tablespoons flour
- 2 eggs

Directions:

1. Select BAKE, set the temperature to 375ºF, and set the time to 10 minutes. Select START/STOP to begin preheating.
2. Grease four ramekins with a little butter.
3. Rigorously combine the eggs, butter, and sugar before stirring in the melted chocolate.
4. Slowly fold in the flour.
5. Spoon an equal amount of the mixture into each ramekin.
6. Put them in the pot. Close the hood and BAKE for 10 minutes.
7. Put the ramekins upside-down on plates and let the cakes fall out. Serve hot.

Grilled Apple Fries With Caramel Cream Cheese Dip

Servings: 4
Cooking Time: 5 Minutes
Ingredients:

- 4 apples, such as Honeycrisp, Gala, Pink Lady, or Granny Smith, peeled, cored, and sliced
- ¼ cup heavy (whipping) cream
- 1 tablespoon granulated sugar
- ¼ teaspoon cinnamon
- ¼ cup all-purpose flour
- 4 ounces cream cheese, at room temperature
- 1 tablespoon caramel sauce
- 1 tablespoon light brown sugar, packed

Directions:

1. Insert the Grill Grate and close the hood. Select GRILL, set the temperature to MAX, and set the time to 5 minutes. Select START/STOP to begin preheating.
2. In a large bowl, toss the apple slices with the heavy cream, granulated sugar, and cinnamon to coat. Slowly shake in the flour and continue mixing to coat.
3. In a small bowl, mix together the cream cheese, caramel sauce, and brown sugar until smooth. Set aside.
4. When the unit beeps to signify it has preheated, place the apples on the Grill Grate in a single layer. Close the hood and grill for 2 minutes, 30 seconds.
5. After 2 minutes, 30 seconds, open the hood and flip and toss the apples around. Close the hood and cook for 2 minutes, 30 seconds more.
6. When cooking is complete, open the hood and remove the apple chips from the grill. Serve with the sauce.

Black Forest Pies

Servings: 6
Cooking Time: 15 Minutes
Ingredients:

- 3 tablespoons milk or dark chocolate chips
- 2 tablespoons thick, hot fudge sauce
- 2 tablespoons chopped dried cherries
- 1 sheet frozen puff pastry, thawed
- 1 egg white, beaten
- 2 tablespoons sugar
- ½ teaspoon cinnamon

Directions:

1. Insert the Crisper Basket and close the hood. Select BAKE, set the temperature to 350ºF, and set the time to 15 minutes. Select START/STOP to begin preheating.
2. In a small bowl, combine the chocolate chips, fudge sauce, and dried cherries.
3. Roll out the puff pastry on a floured surface. Cut into 6 squares with a sharp knife.
4. Divide the chocolate chip mixture into the center of each puff pastry square. Fold the squares in half to make triangles. Firmly press the edges with the tines of a fork to seal.
5. Brush the triangles on all sides sparingly with the beaten egg white. Sprinkle the tops with sugar and cinnamon.
6. Put in the Crisper Basket. Close the hood and BAKE for 15 minutes or until the triangles are golden brown. The filling will be hot, so cool for at least 20 minutes before serving.

Ultimate Skillet Brownies

Servings: 6
Cooking Time: 40 Minutes
Ingredients:

- ½ cup all-purpose flour
- ¼ cup unsweetened cocoa powder
- ¾ teaspoon sea salt
- 2 large eggs
- 1 tablespoon water
- ½ cup granulated sugar
- ½ cup dark brown sugar
- 1 tablespoon vanilla extract
- 8 ounces semisweet chocolate chips, melted
- ¾ cup unsalted butter, melted
- Nonstick cooking spray

Directions:

1. In a medium bowl, whisk together the flour, cocoa powder, and salt.
2. In a large bowl, whisk together the eggs, water, sugar, brown sugar, and vanilla until smooth.
3. In a microwave-safe bowl, melt the chocolate in the microwave. In a separate microwave-safe bowl, melt the butter.
4. In a separate medium bowl, stir together the chocolate and butter until evenly combined. Whisk into the egg mixture. Then slowly add the dry ingredients, stirring just until incorporated.
5. Remove the Grill Grate from the unit. Select BAKE, set the temperature to 350°F, and set the time to 40 minutes. Select START/STOP to begin preheating.
6. Meanwhile, lightly grease the baking pan with cooking spray. Pour the batter into the pan, spreading evenly.
7. When the unit beeps to signify it has preheated, place the pan directly in the pot. Close the hood and BAKE for 40 minutes.
8. After 40 minutes, check that baking is complete. A wooden toothpick inserted into the center of the brownies should come out clean.

Grilled Banana S'mores

Servings: 4
Cooking Time: 6 Minutes
Ingredients:

- 4 large bananas
- 1 cup milk chocolate chips
- 1 cup mini marshmallows
- 4 graham crackers, crushed

Directions:

1. Insert the Cooking Pot and close the hood. Select GRILL, set the temperature to HI, and set the time to 6 minutes. Select START/STOP to begin preheating.
2. While the unit is preheating, prepare the banana boats. Starting at the bottom of a banana, slice the peel lengthwise up one side and then the opposite side. Pull the top half of the peel back, revealing the fruit underneath, but keeping the bottom of the banana peel intact. With a spoon, carefully scoop out some of the banana. (Eat it or set it aside.) Repeat with each banana. Equally divide the chocolate chips and marshmallows between the banana boats.
3. When the unit beeps to signify it has preheated, place the bananas in the Cooking Pot. Close the hood and cook for 6 minutes.
4. When cooking is complete, remove the bananas from the grill and sprinkle the crushed graham crackers on top. Serve.

Apple Pie Crumble

Servings: 4
Cooking Time: 20 Minutes
Ingredients:

- 3 small apples, such as Honeycrisp, Gala, Pink Lady, or Granny Smith, peeled, cored, and cut into ⅛-inch-thick slices
- ¼ cup granulated sugar
- ½ teaspoon cinnamon
- ½ cup quick-cooking oatmeal
- 4 tablespoons (½ stick) unsalted butter, at room temperature
- ½ cup all-purpose flour
- ½ cup light brown sugar, packed

Directions:

1. Insert the Cooking Pot and close the hood. Select GRILL, set the temperature to LO, and set the time to 20 minutes. Select START/STOP to begin preheating.
2. While the unit is preheating, put the apples in a large bowl and coat with the granulated sugar and cinnamon. In a medium bowl, combine the oatmeal, butter, flour, and brown sugar, stirring to make clumps for the top layer.
3. Place the apples in a 6-inch springform pan in an even layer. Spread the oatmeal topping over the apples.
4. When the unit beeps to signify it has preheated, place the pan in the Cooking Pot. Close the hood and cook for 20 minutes.
5. After 20 minutes, open the hood and remove the pan from the unit. The apples should be soft and the topping golden brown. Serve.

Lemony Blackberry Crisp

Servings: 1
Cooking Time: 20 Minutes
Ingredients:

- 2 tablespoons lemon juice
- ⅓ cup powdered erythritol
- ¼ teaspoon xantham gum

- 2 cup blackberries
- 1 cup crunchy granola

Directions:

1. Select BAKE, set the temperature to 350°F, and set the time to 15 minutes. Select START/STOP to begin preheating.
2. In a bowl, combine the lemon juice, erythritol, xantham gum, and blackberries. Transfer to a round baking pan and cover with aluminum foil.
3. Place the pan directly in the pot. Close the hood and BAKE for 12 minutes.
4. Take care when removing the pan from the grill. Give the blackberries a stir and top with the granola.
5. Return the pan to the grill and bake at 320°F for an additional 3 minutes. Serve once the granola has turned brown and enjoy.

Oatmeal And Carrot Cookie Cups

Servings:16
Cooking Time: 8 Minutes
Ingredients:

- 3 tablespoons unsalted butter, at room temperature
- ¼ cup packed brown sugar
- 1 tablespoon honey
- 1 egg white
- ½ teaspoon vanilla extract

- ⅓ cup finely grated carrot
- ½ cup quick-cooking oatmeal
- ⅓ cup whole-wheat pastry flour
- ½ teaspoon baking soda
- ¼ cup dried cherries

Directions:

1. Select BAKE, set the temperature to 350°F, and set the time to 8 minutes. Select START/STOP to begin preheating.
2. In a medium bowl, beat the butter, brown sugar, and honey until well combined.
3. Add the egg white, vanilla, and carrot. Beat to combine.
4. Stir in the oatmeal, pastry flour, and baking soda.
5. Stir in the dried cherries.
6. Double up 32 mini muffin foil cups to make 16 cups. Fill each with about 4 teaspoons of dough. Place the cookie cups directly in the pot.
7. Close the hood and BAKE for 8 minutes, 8 at a time, or until light golden brown and just set. Serve warm.

Chia Pudding

Servings: 2
Cooking Time: 4 Minutes
Ingredients:
- 1 cup chia seeds
- 1 cup unsweetened coconut milk
- 1 teaspoon liquid stevia
- 1 tablespoon coconut oil
- 1 teaspoon butter, melted

Directions:
1. Select BAKE, set the temperature to 360°F, and set the time to 4 minutes. Select START/STOP to begin preheating.
2. Mix together the chia seeds, coconut milk, and stevia in a large bowl. Add the coconut oil and melted butter and stir until well blended.
3. Divide the mixture evenly between the ramekins, filling only about ⅔ of the way. Transfer to the pot.
4. Close the hood and BAKE for 4 minutes.
5. Allow to cool for 5 minutes and serve warm.

Vanilla Scones

Servings:18
Cooking Time: 15 Minutes
Ingredients:
- For the scones
- 2 cups almond flour
- ¼ cup granulated sugar
- ¼ teaspoon salt
- 1 tablespoon baking powder
- 2 large eggs
- 1 teaspoon vanilla extract
- 4 tablespoons (½ stick) unsalted butter, melted
- 2 tablespoons heavy (whipping) cream
- For the icing
- 1 cup powdered sugar
- 2 tablespoons heavy (whipping) cream
- 1 tablespoon vanilla extract

Directions:
1. In a large bowl, combine the almond flour, granulated sugar, salt, and baking powder. In another large bowl, whisk the eggs, then whisk in the vanilla, butter, and heavy cream. Add the dry ingredients to the wet and mix just until a dough forms.
2. Insert the Cooking Pot and close the hood. Select BAKE, set the temperature to 325°F, and set the time to 15 minutes. Select START/STOP to begin preheating.
3. While the unit is preheating, divide the dough into 3 equal pieces. Shape each piece into a disc about 1 inch thick and 5 inches in diameter. Cut each into 6 wedges, like slicing a pizza.
4. When the unit beeps to signify it has preheated, place the scones in the Cooking Pot, spacing them apart so they don't bake together. Close the hood and cook for 15 minutes.
5. While the scones are baking, in a small bowl, combine the powdered sugar, heavy cream, and vanilla. Stir until smooth.
6. After 15 minutes, open the hood and remove the scones. They are done baking when they have turned a light golden brown. Place on a wire rack to cool to room temperature. Drizzle the icing over the scones, or pour a tablespoonful on the top of each scone for an even glaze.

INDEX

A

B

C

Buttermilk Ranch Chicken Tenders 46

Chicken Cordon Bleu Roll-ups 47

Salsa Verde Chicken Enchiladas 51

Stuffed Spinach Chicken Breast 52

Chicken Drumstick

Adobo Chicken 44

Sweet-and-sour Drumsticks 47

Spicy Bbq Chicken Drumsticks 49

Chicken Thighs

Sriracha-honey Glazed Chicken Thighs 40

Ginger Chicken Thighs 41

Cilantro-lime Chicken Thighs 42

Lemon And Rosemary Chicken 43

Herbed Grilled Chicken Thighs 49

Chicken Wing

Buttermilk Marinated Chicken Wings 36

Soy-garlic Crispy Chicken 40

Maple-teriyaki Chicken Wings 46

Crispy Dill Pickle Chicken Wings 51

Chocolate

Chocolate And Peanut Butter Lava Cupcakes 82

Chocolate S'mores 85

Rich Chocolate Cookie 86

Ultimate Coconut Chocolate Cake 89

Chocolate Molten Cake 90

Black Forest Pies 91

Ultimate Skillet Brownies 92

G

H

K

L

M

O

P

R

S

T

W

Y

Z

Made in the USA
Monee, IL
01 December 2024

71541654R00059